ANCHORED

Anchored in God's Word

Scripture that walked me through a Season of Struggle

ALICE R. OWENS

Printed in the United States of America

ISBN 978-0-578-85372-7

www.AnchoredInGodsWord.com

Copyright © 2021 Alice R. Owens

All rights reserved.

ISBN: 978-0-578-85372-7

DEDICATION

This book is dedicated to the memory of my Queen. My Mom Lillian M. Owens.

She accepted Christ at an early age and served, tirelessly and faithfully without complaint.

She planted the seeds of faith, prayer, worship, service, and learning God's Word. She watered and nurtured those seeds to growth for many.

She did not pass through your life – she touched it.

CONTENTS

ACKNOWLEDGMENTS

Heartfelt Thanks are due to:

My siblings, Debbie, Lucky, and Carol for their unconditional love and support.

My children/my crew, Jennifer, Jamal, Aaron, and Arianna for their steady belief, support and keeping me sane with love and laughter.

My former Pastor and First Lady, Pastor Philandrew Miller and Alexis Miller of Humanity Baptist Church for helping me to re-anchor in God's Word.

My current Pastors – Pastor Shaun and Pastor Dianna Nepstad of Fellowship Church for helping me to strengthen my personal relationship with Christ through Small Groups.

My Spiritual Sisters and Brother, Rikesha Dudley Marshall, Lorie Baugh, Vanessa Babauta and Sean Fields for their prayers and support.

My Spiritual Rings – Romesa Wilson (Desperately Seeking Jesus), Dannielle Hart (God's Hart), ReGina Duncan (The Living Room), Pastor Kim Moreno (Women of Worth), Carrie Kikes (Daughters of the King), and Nancy Akins (The Watering Hole), for being an encouraging network of spiritual builders in God's Kingdom.

Special thank you to Jamal for cover editing and talking me through my emotional and mental stress moments.

Finally, eternal thanks, unconditional love, and praise and glory to God my Father for being with me through my Season of Struggle, giving me this assignment and placing His trust in me to follow through.

My Season – The Perfect Storm

My season began in 2009 and lasted 10 years. I call it the Perfect Storm. It had two halves – before and after. Before was when I drifted from God. After was when I re-anchored in God's Word. It was a season that was created by what I call the perfect storm – finances, health, family, and career issues all occurring at the same time.

It was a season filled with stress, self-hatred, sadness, rejection, and fear. I experienced loss of family, home, health, finances and career.

I grew up in the Baptist Church. I served many years in the church in many ways. It was like an act of duty – I joined the church and was baptized. I prayed, read the bible, worshiped and served. However, there was no personal relationship with Christ. My relationships were with the spiritual leaders of each auxiliary and the Pastors. So, when my Pastors were called home and leaders went to other churches, I too left.

I drifted away from church and away from God. I began going through life without Christ. I became an "as needed" Christian. I read my bible (as needed), l listened to gospel music (as needed), and I prayed (as needed). I had my job, my apartment, my health, my family, my career. Life was good. I was the "I believe in God, pray when I need Him, Easter, Mother's Day and Christmas Services Christian." Then, my perfect storm hit. And no George Clooney was not involved.

Health issues, hostile work environment, financial struggles, broken relationships, rising debt, etc. The storm was a tidal wave that hit me emotionally, mentally, physically, and financially. I felt fear, anxiety, shame, guilt, anger, self-hatred, resentment, worthlessness and loneliness. I then became the "Victim Christian". The – God, where are you? How could you leave me? Why don't you love me?

Christian.

Proverbs 3:5-6 tells us – *Trust in the LORD with all your heart; do not depend on your own understanding. Seek his will in all you do, and he will show you which path to take.* I did the exact opposite. I did not seek God's trust. I did not seek God's guidance. I thought I knew everything. I tried to fix what I could in any way that I could and if I made it through the day – hallelujah! Unfortunately, I did not fix much. I added to the problems.

The problems became so overwhelming, thoughts of suicide took over. I began to think how my death would be a relief – not just for me but also for those whom my problems had touched. What a thought! That my family and friends would welcome my death.

Then one day, while with my Mom, she noticed how lifeless I was and told me it was time to stop drifting and time to re-anchor. Re-anchor myself in God's Word. As she put it, "go to the well and drink the Living Water."

She directed me to *Jeremiah 29:11 – For I know the plans I have for you, says the LORD. They are plans for good and not for disaster, to give you a future and a hope.*

She instructed me to study God's Word not read it. Because there is a huge difference. God's Word cannot be read like a novel. It must be studied as the blueprint for the life God wants us to live.

I was still in my season, but the re-anchoring had begun. I pressed into God's Word and discovered Scripture that would help me to understand, manage and survive my Season of Struggle.

It is in obedience to God's instruction that I now share those Scriptures with you.

It is my prayer that as you read this book, you are moved to open God's Word and began Anchoring.

Faith

Those who know your name trust in you, for you O LORD, do not abandon those who search for you.
Psalm 9:10

Replace Your Fear

But when I am afraid, I will put my trust in you. I praise God for what he has promised. I trust in God, so why should I be afraid? What can mere mortals do to me?
Psalm 56:3-4

At some time in our life, we all face something that makes us afraid.

My greatest fear was losing our family home. I dreaded going to the mailbox, receiving a phone call or even a knock at the door.

I had to replace fear and anxiety with faith and trust in God. *Psalm 56:10-11* tells us – *I praise God for what he has promised; yes, I praise the LORD for what he has promised. I trust in God, so why should I be afraid? What can mere mortals do to me?* What can man do to us? Nothing! Mortal man and his evil ways have no power over us.

When we place our trust in God, we are under His protection. Fear and anxiety are eliminated. Human nature from others may continue to be mean spirited but it cannot break us.

Scripture tells us – *The LORD is for me, so I will have no fear. What can mere people do to me? (Psalm 118:6)*. Stand confident in God's ability to do all things. Have belief that God is almighty and faith that God is on His Throne.

As I anchored myself in God's Word – little by little my anxiety level lowered. My fear started to dissolve. Confidence. Belief. Faith. These words replaced fear, anxiety, worry.

Fear has no place in our walk with Christ.

Declaration: Declare today, fear has no place in my walk with Christ. Replace your fear and anxiety with faith and trust in God.

Action: Study on God's Word. Meditate on scriptures on belief and faith.

Prayer: Lord, I replace my fear with faith and trust in You. Fear has no place in my walk with Christ. I stand on Your Word and declare – In God I Trust! Man can do nothing to me! In Jesus Name. Amen

Tell God All

O my people, trust I him at all times.
Pour out your heart to him, for God is our refuge.
Psalm 62:8

I talk with God all the time. When I'm cleaning, shopping, walking. Anytime and anywhere.

The conversations we think we can have with no one – we can have with God. It does not matter the situation. We can talk to God at anytime and anywhere. God is our shelter, protection, safety and security. He is also our friend, confidant, and counselor.

Scripture tells us in *Philippians 4:6 – Don't worry about anything; instead, pray about everything. Tell God what you need, and thank him for all he has done.* This is the de-stress scripture! We can seek his advice, tell him our problems, share our fears. We can be open, honest and leave it all with Him.

Pour out your heart. Open your mouth and speak freely to God. Tell him all! Let go! Release!

Declaration: Declare today, I am a Child of God and I am blessed to have a Father who listens.

Action: Study on God's Word. Meditate on scriptures on talking to God. Start your day with "Good Morning Father" and have that conversation with Him. Go to Him, talk to Him, leave it with Him.

Prayer: Lord, I come to You with an open heart speaking freely to

You my Father. Thank You for hearing my cry. Father, I pour out my heart before You. Telling You all and leaving it all with You. You are a God of compassion and wisdom. You are my shelter in the time of storm. You fight my battles as I keep still. Father, I trust You in all things. In Jesus Name. Amen

Hiding Place

For you are my hiding place; you protect me from trouble.
You surround me with songs of victory.
Psalm 32:7

W hen the stresses of life come at you and they will – go to God.

He is our hiding place. *Psalm 121:7* tells us- *The LORD keeps you from all harm and watches over your life.* From all manners of evil – problems, stress, worry, deception, etc. God is our place of protection. If it is not of God and from God, it will not touch us.

When we shelter-in-place with God, we are enclosed in His hedge of protection. We are in His Presence. No one and nothing can breach God's stronghold.

Scripture tells us we can rest in knowing that God is not only protecting us from trouble but He has already handled the situation and we will come out of it with shouts of praise.

Psalm 40:3 – He has given me a new song to sing, a hymn of praise to our God. Many will see what he has done and be amazed. They will put their trust in the LORD.

Our emergence from our hiding place with God, will bring joy to us in the morning. Others will witness and see what God has done in our life and place their trust in God. Our testimony may be someone else's breakthrough.

Declaration: Declare today, God is my refuge from all storms of life.

Action: Study on God's Word. Meditate on scriptures on refuge.

Prayer: Lord, You are my hiding place. I thank You for Your shelter in the time of my storms. I thank You for Your hedge of protection. Father, I rest in You knowing that I will come out of this situation with shouts of praise. When life hits me, I will run to God and remain in Your presence. May my testimony of Your love, mercy and grace lead others to Your trust. In Jesus Name. Amen

Let God Carry You

Praise the LORD; praise God our savior!
For each day he carries us in his arms.
Psalm 68:19

As I study on this scripture – I close my eyes and visualize when I was a child: I have fallen, I look up and my father is standing there, arms extended. As with my earthly father, my heavenly Father is waiting, arms extended, to lift me and carry me.

Life can be frustrating, tiring, draining, exhausting. It affects all areas of wellness: social, emotional, mental, financial, physical, spiritual, environmental, occupational. It releases a tidal wave of emotions.

We try to be so many things for so many people in so many ways – it's exhausting. We try to do so many things for so many people in so many ways – it's draining.

So, when life presses in – we need to press in - into our Father. Scripture tells us to go to Him - *Matthew 11:28 – Then Jesus said, Come to me, all of you who are weary and carry heavy burdens, and I will give you rest.*

Run to our Father and let Him carry you. Close your eyes and climb into His waiting arms.

Declaration: Declare today, that God is my source of rest, renewal, refreshing, restoration, recovery, healing.

Action: Study God's Word. Meditate on scriptures on rest, renewal, restoration, healing.

Prayer: LORD, thank You for catching me when I stumble, picking me up when I fall and carrying me when I cannot take another step. Father, You are my deliverer, my redeemer; my strength and salvation. In You I seek rest and restoration. In Jesus Name. Amen

Never Alone

Those who know your name trust in you, for you, O LORD, do not abandon those who search for you.
Psalm 9:10

There were times in my season where it seemed as if I had been abandoned. I looked around and I wondered – where has everyone gone? Human nature drives some people to disappear when the going gets tough.

Others may leave you. But God has not forgotten you. And faith is knowing God is there.

Though you may not see Him, you are not alone.
Though you may not hear Him, you are not alone.
Though you may not feel Him, you are not alone.

Psalm 94:14 (ESV) – For the LORD will not forsake his people; he will not abandon his heritage.

I drifted from God – He did not drift away from me. No matter how far away from God you feel know that He is there. We are His people. His legacy. No matter what we are going through, no matter what we do – God will never leave us.

Learn His name, know His name – trust Him.

Declaration: Declare today, that no matter what life throws at me, I am never alone. I am God's legacy and He will never leave me.

Action: Study on God's Word. Meditate on scriptures on God's

Presence.

Prayer: LORD, though I may not see You, though I may not hear You, though I may not feel You – I am not alone. I know Your name; I seek You and I put my trust in You. In Jesus Name. Amen

No Hiding Place

even there your hand will guide me, and your strength will support me.
Psalm 139:10

The theme for *Psalm 139 (ESV)* is *"Search Me, O God, and Know my Heart"*

In *Psalm 139:2-9*, David is talking to God and acknowledging God is everywhere. He knows all, sees all and holds all power. We are never out of his reach. There is no hiding place.

When I drifted from God, I was ashamed to turn and run back to Him. I did not understand as David did in *Psalm 139:1 – O LORD, you have examined my heart and know everything about me.* God already knew.

He knows. Our thoughts, our dreams, our hopes, our fears. He knows our comings and our goings. You can fool all the people some of the time and some of the time and some of the people all the time. However, you cannot fool God ever! What you do in secret is not a secret from God.

God himself declares in *Jeremiah 23:23-24 – Am I a God who is only close at hand? says the LORD. "No, I am far away at the same time. Can anyone hide from me in a secret place? Am I not everywhere in all the heavens and earth?" says the LORD.*

I could not hide from God. You cannot hide from God. Why would we want to? What sins have we committed that He has not already forgiven? What unspoken thought, that He does not already know? Where can our footsteps fall that God has not already been?

Continue to seek God. Stay committed and faithful.

Declaration: Declare today, I have no secret places to hide from God. I run to Him every day.

Action: Study God's Word. Meditate on *Psalm 139 Search me, O God, and Know My Heart (ESV)*.

Prayer: LORD, thank You for being present wherever I may go. LORD, I have no secret place where You may not see me. Thank You for leading me and sustaining me each day. Keep me under Your watchful eye. Search me, know me, keep me. In Jesus Name. Amen

Unconditional Faith

Faith shows the reality of what we hope for; it is the evidence of things we cannot see.
Hebrews 11:1

Hebrews 11(ESV) is the *By Faith* chapter. I love this chapter. I call it the Faith Hall of Fame.

Abel, Enoch, Noah, Abraham, Sarah,
Isaac, Jacob, Moses, People of Israel, Rahab,
Gideon, Barak, Samson, Jephthah,
David, Samuel, the Prophets

By faith Abel offered to God a more acceptable sacrifice than Cain. *Hebrews 11:4*

By faith Enoch was taken up so that he should not see death, and he was not found, because God had taken him. *Hebrews 11:5*

By faith Noah constructed an ark for the saving of his household. *Hebrews 11:7*

By faith Abraham obeyed when he was called to go out to a place that he was to receive as an inheritance. *Hebrews 11:8*

By faith Sarah received power to conceive. *Hebrews 11:11*

By faith Abraham, when tested, offered up Isaac. *Hebrews 11:17*

By faith Isaac invoked future blessings on Jacob and Esau. *Hebrews 11:20*

14

By faith Jacob, blessed each of the sons of Joseph. *Hebrews 11:21*

By faith Joseph, at the end of his life, made mention of the exodus of the Israelites and gave directions concerning his bones. *Hebrews 11:22*

By faith Moses, was hidden for three months by his parents. *Hebrews 11:23*

By faith Moses, refused to be called the son of Pharaoh's daughter. *Hebrews 11:24*

By faith the People of Israel, crossed the Red Sea. *Hebrews 11:29*

All had faith. Unconditional trust and belief in God. Belief that He is who He says He is. Trust that He would do as He promised. As you go through your season – this is the type of faith that must be established. Unconditional Faith.

We were given this hope when we were saved. (If we already have something, we don't need to hope for it. But if we look forward to something we don't yet have, we must wait patiently and confidently.) Romans 8:24-25

Our hope rests in knowing that although we do not see the things God is doing, we know He is working on our behalf. We trust in His word and we stand on His promises - He is with us, He loves us, He provides for us, He protects us, He strengthens us and He is in control.

Declaration: Declare today, I have unconditional faith in God and I am a Faith Walker.

Action: Study God's Word. Meditate on *Hebrews 11–Faith Chapter*. Step out on faith and put your trust in God.

Prayer: Lord, I step out on faith and put my trust in You. As You were with Abel, Enoch, Noah, Abraham, Sarah, Isaac, Jacob, Joseph, Moses, You are with me. By faith, I will obey when You call. By faith, I commit my life to You. By faith, I will go where You send me. By faith, I stand on Your promises. In Jesus Name. Amen

God Meets Our Needs

And this same God who takes care of me will supply all your needs from his glorious riches, which have been given to us in Christ Jesus.

Philippians 4:19

As I was going through my season, God was providing me with what I needed, not the things I wanted.

I wanted a miracle of funds to catch-up my mortgage. He provided a good attorney that helped me with my bankruptcy.

I wanted a new job to escape my hostile work environment. He provided a hedge of protection to shelter me from job loss.

God humbled me. He showed me that it does not always take a miracle to overcome a bad situation. He gave me what I needed - learnings. Learnings to sustain me and help me in the future. I needed to learn to be responsible with my finances. I needed to learn not to run from difficulties.

2 Corinthians 9:8 tells us – *And God will generously provide all you need. Then you will have everything you need and plenty left over to share with others.*

The bankruptcy took seven years, but it saved my home. It also started me to be mindful of budgeting and work towards financial stability. I was able to sell the home and share the funds with my siblings. Today, I am 80% debt free. He provided me with patience and endurance to meet my obligation for seven years.

I remained on the job. I focused on the responsibilities of my position and not the hostile environment. The hostile employee was dismissed; I received a promotion; was able to train others to move forward in their careers. Today, I am retired. Spending time in God's Word. He provided me with strength and courage to face a difficult situation.

I needed to learn the difference between my wants and needs. I needed to learn that God will supply my every need and provide overflow to bless others. I needed to learn that God knows best.

Stand firm in God's Word – He will supply your every need.

Declaration: Declare today, I am blessed each day to know all my needs are supplied.

Action: Study God's Word. Meditate on scriptures on God meeting your needs.

Prayer: Lord, thank You for supplying my every need. Thank You for teaching me the difference between my wants and my needs. Thank You for teaching me to be patient in times of trouble; to be strong when faced with adversity; and to have courage when faced with fear. Favor me Father with overflow that I may continue to bless others. In Jesus Name. Amen

You Are Not Alone

No one will be able to stand against you as long as you live. For I will be with you as I was with Moses. I will not fail you or abandon you.
Joshua 1:5

Storms of life, difficult people, temptations, challenges, daily life, anxiety, fear. We face these things every day. However, God promises and double downs on His promise – *"He will never leave us or abandon us."*

Seasons come with many different situations. You may be in a season of joy and blessings. You may be in a season of storms ranging from minor to major. You may be in a season of confusion and uncertainty. My season was a combination of mild to strong winds, waves of emotions, tornadoes that hit and missed.

It wasn't until I anchored myself in God's Word that I learned – God was with me through the first part of my season and would continue to be with me my entire season.

As God was with me, He is also with you. Knowing God is with us, allows us to live with the attitude of Victory. No one and nothing can oppose us. Difficult coworkers, unpleasant encounters, anxiety, fear, even judgment from fellow believers – God is with us.

Deuteronomy 31:6 tells us – So be strong and courageous! Do not be afraid and do not panic before them. For the LORD your God will personally go ahead of you. He will neither fail you nor abandon you.

He will never abandon us. He will never fail to help us. Seasons will come and go. God will always be with us.

When seasons come – give thanks. Give thanks for the challenges that draw you nearer to God. Give thanks for the blessings and His favor.

Declaration: Declare today, I am not alone. God is with me always.

Action: Study God's Word. Meditate on scriptures on God's Presence.

Prayer: Lord, I am so glad that trouble does not last always. Seasons will come and seasons will go, but You Father are steadfast and true. I hold to Your hand as I walk through my season, thankful I am not alone. In Jesus Name. Amen

Faith and Trust

Trust in the LORD with all your heart; do not depend on your own understanding. Seek his will in all you do, and he will show you which path to take.
Proverbs 3:5-6

When I was in my season, I did the exact opposite of this scripture. I added to the problems I already had. In some instances, I made them worse than they had to be. I thought I knew everything about everything. I tried to fix what I could and if I made it through the day – hallelujah! Unfortunately, I did not fix much.

As I studied on this scripture, I came to see it as a command and an opportunity to be obedient. Trust in the LORD. Do not rely on my own understanding. Acknowledge God always.

Now when things arise in my life – I meditate on this scripture and I do three things – first, I thank God for all He has done in my life. Second, I seek His guidance and trust His instruction. Third, I tell my situation about the God I serve - my God who is trusting and faithful; my God who guides me in all areas of my life.

Commit everything you do to the LORD. Trust him, and he will help you. Psalm 37:5

In this world today, there are so many outside influences that affect our thoughts, reasoning and actions. We must look to God with total faith; trusting in God's guidance, love, and understanding. Standing firm with Christ in our heart and all areas of our life – submitting to His will and seeking His guidance in everything. He will direct us and show us the way to go.

I came through my season and I learned to have faith; trust in God; acknowledge and admit my belief; be dedicated in my work; submit to God's will; commit my life to God.

Stand firm with Christ in your heart and all areas of your life.

Declaration: Declare today, I stand firm in faith and trust in Christ.

Action: Study God's Word. Meditate on scriptures on faith and trust.

Prayer: Lord, in this world today, there are so many outside influences that affect my thoughts, reasoning and actions. Lord I look to You with total faith, trusting in Your guidance, love and understanding. Lord I stand firm with You in my heart and all areas of my life. Lord, make my paths straight. In Jesus Name. Amen

Do Not Bend

The temptations in your life are no different from what others experience. And God is faithful. He will not allow the temptation to be more than you can stand. When you are tempted, he will show you a way out so that you can endure.
1 Corinthians 10:13

Temptation is defined as the desire to do something, especially something wrong or unwise. It is a thing or course of action that attracts or tempts someone.

Throughout my season, I faced temptation. I was tempted to apply for quick loans to help with debt. I was tempted to leave a tenured position to be rid of a hostile work environment. I was tempted to eat the quick fast foods jeopardizing my health.

We face temptations every day at every moment in our lives. Temptations are both big and small. To eat unhealthily, play hooky from work, gossip about others, skip a workout, not go to church, etc.

Don't be fooled. The temptations we face are seedings from the enemy. The enemy counts on us to pick up that seed and give in to the temptation instead of going to God in prayer for deliverance from the temptation. The enemy knows we are blessed to have a God who is faithful. A Father who will not allow us to be tempted with things that are too much for us to handle.

My debt was a burden. The work environment was toxic. My health was fragile. Through faith, trust and prayer, our Father gave me a way to break free and continue on. He provided an attorney to guide me through debt reconciliation; new management to provide strong workplace leadership; new nutritionist to provide healthy guidelines.

Temptations will entice us but when the enemy drops those seeds, step over them and keep on walking with Christ.

Declaration: Declare today, I will not bend to the enemy's temptations. I will remain in Christ.

Action: Study God's Word. Meditate on scriptures on dealing with temptations.

Prayer: Thank You Lord for not letting me be tempted beyond my capacity. When the enemy drops his seeds of temptations, let me not bend and pick them up. When I am tempted, provide me a way to break free and tolerance to not break. In Jesus Name. Amen

Trust God's Character

God is not a man, so he does not lie.
He is not human, so he does not change his mind.
Has he ever spoken and failed to act?
Has he ever promised and not carried it through?
Numbers 23:19

W hen I don't understand the why, the what, the where, or the who of any situation – I trust God knows.

God keeps His word. He does not lie. He does not go back on His word. If He speaks it – He will do it. If He promised it – He will fulfill it. God has no reason to deceive us. What would God achieve by breaking a promise?

The grass withers and the flowers fade, but the word of our God stands forever. Isaiah 40:8

People and public opinions will always change. A person will go back on their word in the blink of an eye. The Word of God stands forever. It is consistent as is God – yesterday, today and tomorrow. In *Exodus 34:6-7 (ESV)*, God himself described His character – The LORD passed before him and proclaimed, *The LORD, the LORD, a God merciful and gracious, slow to anger, and abounding in steadfast love, and faithfulness, keeping steadfast love for thousands, forgiving iniquity and transgression and sin.*

You may not know why a situation has occurred – Trust God

You may not know what the plan is – Trust God

You may not foresee the outcome – Trust God

Trust God's character. He does not lie. He does not change His mind. He keeps His word.

Declaration: Declare today, I stand firm on my trust in God.

Action: Study God's Word. Meditate on scriptures on God's Character.

Prayer: LORD, I agree with Paul – *"I don't want to be bothered anymore. I have far more important things to do – the serious living of this faith"*. And that faith includes trusting Your character. You are not man, that You would lie or change Your mind. Your Word never changes. I stand firm in my trust in You. In Jesus Name. Amen

Advocating for God

Fight the good fight for the true faith.
Hold tightly to the eternal life to which God has called you, which
you have declared so well before many witnesses.
1 Timothy 6:12

W hat are you doing for God? Are you His champion? Do you defend His name, His character? Are you God's Advocate?

We were born children of God. When we accepted and moved forward in Confession of Christ in our life – we became His champion. His advocate. We accepted the assignment God called us to. We accepted the responsibility of publicly supporting His Faith. It is not a temporary assignment, it is forever.

To be an advocate for God:
• Place God first in your life
• Stand firm in your belief in God
• Study God's Word
• Become established in the life God has assigned you
• Sharpen your spiritual gifts to use for God's purpose
• Ask God to give you voice to testify and share with others your life in Christ
• Be strong and eliminate from your life that which is not pleasing to God and cannot be used in service to God
• Surround yourself with fellow Champions of Christ
• Do God's work – go where God leads you
• Be obedient
• Always seek God's face
• Stay in prayer

Where do you stand? Are you on God's side?

Be an advocate for God. Champion God's Word.

Declaration: Declare today, I am an Advocate for God, a Champion of Christ, and a Guardian of the Faith.

Action: Study God's Word. Meditate on scriptures on championing God.

Prayer: Lord, I am on Your side. Strengthen me to fight the good fight and run my race. I keep to my faith and stand as a Champion of Your Word. In Jesus Name. Amen

Live God's Word

But don't just listen to God's word. You must do as it says.
Otherwise, you are only fooling yourselves.
James 1:22

At the lowest point in my season, when I was ready to give up, my Mother directed me back to God's Word to anchor myself with scripture.

As I studied God's Word, I came upon this scripture. I love *The Message* translation: *Don't fool yourself into thinking that you are a listener when you are anything but, letting the Word go in one ear and out the other. Act on what you hear! (James 1:22/MSG)*

Don't just read the word – live it!

Our time in God's Word should have an effect on our attitudes and our behavior. As we read God's Word, we must also open our eyes to see, our ears to hear and our hearts to obey. If we are going to talk about God's Word, then we must also walk out God's Word. We have to live it.

Jesus tells us in *Matthew 7:26*: *But anyone who hears my teaching and doesn't obey it is foolish, like a person who builds a house on sand*. Why study God's Word and not follow it?

As I studied scriptures on faith, I realized I had to walk out that faith. I had to turn my belief into faith and then strengthen that faith with trust. I had to give up. And so, I did.

I gave up to God. I let go of self and took hold of God. I submitted all to Him. My life, my family, my home, my job, my health, my struggles. I let go and let God have His way.

Our belief in God must turn into faith in God. Don't just study God's Word – Live it!

Declaration: Declare today, I am Anchored in God's Word. I don't just study God's Word – I live it!

Action: Study God's Word. Meditate on *James 1:19-27 Listening and Doing*.

Prayer: Lord, thank You for opening my eyes to see, my ears to hear, my heart and soul to understand. Holy Spirit, guide me each day to live God's Word – letting go of self and taking hold of Your Word. In Jesus Name. Amen

Place of Victory

And who can win this battle against the world?
Only those who believe that Jesus is the Son of God
1 John 5:5

Christ has already overcome this world and our faith in Christ = Victory.

As *1 John 5:4* tells us: *For every child of God defeats this evil world, and we achieve this victory through our faith.*

As I studied on these scriptures, I felt a sense of relief come upon me. I still had the same problems but I no longer felt defeated. My attitude shifted. I begin to see light at the end of the tunnel. I could see bills marked paid, health improving, job stress fading. I begin to look at things from a place of victory.

Don't give up! No matter how small or big the battle. When the enemy attacks and the world comes at us – we can face whatever is thrown at us.

As children of God, we are already in a place of victory Our faith defeats both the world and the enemy.

Declaration: Declare today, I come from a place of Victory. Christ has overcome this world.

Action: Study God's Word. Meditate on *1 John 5 God is life.*

Prayer: Lord, I am blessed to come from a place of victory when the enemy and the world come at me. By the blood shed on the cross,

Christ overcame this world and gave us the victory. Whatever I may go through, the victory is mine. I have overcome this world and the enemy. In Jesus Name. Amen

Get Anchored

But when you ask him, be sure that your faith is in God alone. Do not waver, for a person with divided loyalty is as unsettled as a wave of the sea that is blown and tossed by the wind.
James 1:6

This scripture describes me perfectly during the first half of my season.

I would ask God for help, while at the same time doubting, He would come through. I was blown and tossed going from one thing to another with nothing working. I was not anchored so I was blown far offshore.

When I drifted away from Christ, it was an open invitation for the enemy to send storm clouds my way. The enemy will use any little opening to gain a foothold into your situation. And he did.

Jesus tells us in *Matthew 21:22* that *you can pray for anything, and if you have faith, you will receive it*. As I became anchored in God's Word, my belief turned into faith and my faith led to trust. The storm levels shifted and I was making my way back to shore. There were still high winds and rough waves, but I was now anchored.

My asks became prayers. Prayers acknowledging God as my Father; thankfulness for His guidance; praise and worship for Him accepting me for all my sins and failures; forgiveness for my divided loyalty. There were times when my prayers did not include any asks. I was grateful to be back on shore.

I have no doubt that God will see me through.

Get anchored. Stay focused on God. Be not divided in your loyalty.

Declaration: Declare today, I am anchored in God's Word. I have no doubt that God will see me through.

Action: Study God's Word. Meditate on *Matthew 21:18-22 Jesus Says the Disciples Can Pray for Anything.*

Prayer: Lord, thank You for Your Word. It keeps me anchored in faith and trust. Your Word draws me in. It teaches me, it challenges me, it makes me think, it makes me question the way of the world. Your Word guides me through each day. Open my eyes to see, my ears to hear, my heart, mind and soul to understand and continue to be fed from Your Word. In Jesus Name. Amen

Four Ways to Fight the Enemy

Be on guard. Stand firm in the faith.
Be courageous. Be strong.
1 Corinthians 16:13

This scripture gives us four ways to fight off the enemy and make it through the day.

Post it on your mirror so you see it each day. It is a daily reminder that at all times we need to be aware.

1. Be on guard. The enemy does not rest. He is slinging darts and arrows, planting seeds of temptations every day. He will use every tactic to come at us.

2. Stand firm in the faith. The enemy is the father of lies. He loves to rob you of your faith by planting feelings of doubt, being unworthy, unloved, etc.

3. Be courageous. Fear has no place in our walk with God. We need courage to face challenges that come our way.

4. Be strong. Strength gives us the ability to deal with situations that arise each day. Both mental and spiritual strength to handle the difficulties of daily life.

Ephesians 6:10 tells us – *Be strong in the LORD and in his mighty power*.

As children of God, we will constantly be tested and challenged because of our faith.

Attacks will come when we least expect it. They may come from family and friends; at work or in social settings; from fellow believers and non-believers. We must stay alert. Rooted in faith. Walking fearless with God. Strong in God's unmatched power.

Declaration: Declare today, I stand firm in my faith and walk fearless with God. I can defeat the enemy.

Action: Study God's Word. Meditate on *1 Corinthians 16:13*.

Prayer: Lord, keep me always on alert, standing firm in the gospel. The enemy will attack at every turn. Give me courage and strength to fight off all attacks that come my way. I call on Your mighty power. In Jesus Name. Amen

Be a Faith Walker

for we walk by faith, not by sight
2 Corinthians 5:7 (ESV)

At a time when I was facing having to make a tough decision that would have a huge impact on all areas of my life – I went Faith Walking!

Faith Walking (my definition): Submitting to God's Will. Giving God complete control. Entering into prayer, seeking His Will on all decisions to be made. Listening to His answer; being obedient in accepting and following His direction when He answers. Being grateful for all victories, blessings, challenges, trials, and tribulations.

After years of being with my company (20+), I was notified my position was being eliminated. I could stay in a lesser position, with more work and a decrease in salary or I could take a severance package. I was in shock!

Funny thing, the shock only lasted a few minutes. There were no tears, no panic, no anxiety. No woe is me; no doom and gloom; no overreaction. Something inside was telling me – you're going to be okay.

I went into my room, bent my knees and went into prayer. I thanked God for the amazing career with the company; thanked Him for bringing me through challenges on the job; thanked Him for former managers, good teammates, wonderful opportunities I had received. I prayed for other coworkers who were facing the same decision. I thanked Him for the transition I would be going through and asked

Him to prepare me for days ahead.

Now I have had my sleepless nights, but that night I slept like a baby. I woke up the next day refreshed, renewed, re-energized, refocused. I had absolutely no idea what lay ahead in the days to come. I put my trust and faith in God's guidance. I gave Him all control and submitted all to Him. I asked Him to lead me to where He would have me to go.

In *Jeremiah 29:11* God tells us – *For I know the plans I have for you, says the LORD, they are plans for good and not for disaster, to give you a future and a hope.*

I did not know it then, but I know it now – this was the last straw to drop into my season of struggle. Like a true test of faith.

I am here to tell you that since I have moved forward in faith and trust in my Father, there has not been a day of worry. I have been blessed with PROMOTION – INCREASE – FAVOR. I put all my trust in my Savior.

Faith is not seeing but fully believing. Take that first step and start walking! Take one step of faith at a time.

It's what we trust in but don't yet see that keeps us going. 2 Corinthians 5:7 (MSG)

Declaration: Declare today, I am a Faith Walker. I place all my trust in God and I walk by faith, not by sight.

Action: Study God's Word. Meditate on scriptures on Faith.

Prayer: Lord, I place all my trust in You. Help me to take that first step of faith. Holy Spirit teach me to be a Faith Walker. LORD, keep me on the path of Faith. In Jesus Name. Amen

Love

Love is patient and kind. Love is not jealous or boastful or proud, or rude. It does not demand its own way. It is not irritable, and it keeps no record of being wronged. It does not rejoice about injustice but rejoices whenever the truth wins out. Love never gives up, never loses faith, is always hopeful, and endures through every circumstance. Prophecy and speaking in unknown languages and special knowledge will become useless. But love will last forever.
1 Corinthians 13:4-8

Listen for God's Voice

Let me hear of your unfailing love each morning, for I am trusting you. Show me where to walk, for I give myself to you.
Psalm 143:8

During my season, a fitful night of sleep was followed with waking up dreading the day.

Quieting yourself is not easy. Turning off the mental "to do list" is difficult. You have to get ready for work, get the kids off to school, you even think about what's for dinner and you haven't eaten breakfast!

When I studied on this scripture, I realized in order to hear God's voice I had to learn to quiet myself.

Notice the scripture pinpoints – *each morning*. This scripture is the template for a new morning routine. Begin your day by quieting your mind and listen for God's voice. Follow the way He has for you to go.

Proverbs 3:5-6 is God's promise to guide our steps – *Trust in the LORD with all your heart, and do not depend on your own understanding. Seek his will in all you do, and he will show you which path to take.* Be assured that where your footsteps fall, God has already been.

As scripture tells us in *Psalm 32:8*, He is teacher, coach, mentor, counselor, watchful eye. *The LORD says, "I will guide you along the best pathway for your life. I will advise you and watch over you.*

Quiet yourself in the morning. Listen for His voice and ask God to show you the way to go.

Declaration: Declare today, God's love is loyal, faithful, committed. He will never lead me to a place where He has not prepared me to go.

Action: Study God's Word. Meditate on *Psalm 143 My Soul Thirsts for You (ESV)*

Prayer: Lord, in the morning when I rise, quiet my mind and let me hear Your voice of love. In all I do today, let me seek You to guide my footsteps. In You Lord I have full trust. In Jesus Name. Amen

Steadfast Love

But I trust in your unfailing love.
I will rejoice because you have rescued me.
Psalm 13:5

S teadfast love is God's description of himself.

God proclaimed it to Moses in *Exodus 34:6 – The LORD passed in front of Moses, calling out, "Yahweh!" The LORD! The God of compassion and mercy! I am slow to anger and filled with unfailing love and faithfulness."*

What an amazing love! God's love is the foundation of our faith. His love is pure, loyal, faithful, merciful. As God's love for us is steadfast and unfailing, so our love for Him must be unfailing and steadfast.

Re-anchoring myself in God's Word taught me that we cannot give up on God because we know God will not give up on us. I have learned that whatever I am going through in life, when I stand firm in my trust and faith in God, His love will carry me through and His salvation rescues me.

Do not give up! Trust in God's steadfast love and He will bring you through.

Declaration: Declare today, I stand firm in my trust and faith in God. His love will carry me through and His salvation rescues me.

Action: Study God's Word. Meditate on scriptures on God's Love.

Prayer: Lord, thank You for Your steadfast love. I trust and stand firm in my faith and Your love for me. Your love is pure, loyal, faithful and merciful. I rejoice in knowing that whatever life throws my way, You are with me. Your love never fails. In Jesus Name. Amen

Chosen to Produce

You didn't choose me. I chose you.
I appointed you to go and produce lasting fruit, so that the Father
will give you whatever you ask for, using my name.
John 15:16

Before I was born, before I was a thought in my parents' mind – I was chosen by Christ. Christ chose me to love, to teach, to fight for and to die for.

We were not chosen to elevate ourselves by declaring "I am the Chosen One". We were chosen to glorify God and declare "I am a chosen one of many". We are not chosen for appearance sake – we are chosen AND appointed to go forward and produce lasting fruit. Christ tells us in *John 15:1: I am the true grapevine and my Father is the gardener.* Christ goes on to tell us in *John 15:5: Yes, I am the vine; you are the branches. Those who remain in me, and I in them, will produce much fruit. For apart from me you can do nothing.*

Through the first half of my season, I was a fractured branch dangling from the vine. And with the fracture I experienced pain, weakness, trauma. I had to anchor myself in God's Word to begin healing that fracture because I could do nothing. I had to learn that God is the gardener – planting, pruning, cultivating. Christ is the grapevine – a single vine supporting many branches. I was the branch – growing from the love of Christ.

I had to submit, commit and accept the pruning of my branch. I had to remain in Christ so that I could begin healing and producing good fruit.

Fruits of the Spirit as told to us in *Galatians 5:22-23*: *But the Holy Spirit produces this kind of fruit in our lives: love, joy, peace, patience, kindness, goodness, faithfulness, gentleness, and self-control.*

Christian Qualities as told to us in *2 Peter 1:5-8*: *In view of all this, make every effort to respond to God's promises. Supplement your faith with a generous provision of moral excellence, and moral excellence with knowledge, and knowledge with self-control, and self-control with patient endurance, and patient endurance with godliness, and godliness with brotherly affection, and brotherly affection with love for everyone. The more you grow like this, the more productive and useful you will be in your knowledge of our Lord Jesus Christ.*

Christ selected us first and decided that we should have thoughts, words, and deeds that are aligned to the Fruits of the Spirit and of Christian quality. In obedience to Christ, it is our responsibility to supply and provide to others the fruit that grows on our branches. With that obedience comes the promise that no matter what we ask of God, in Christ name, He will give to us.

Remain in Christ. Tend to your branch daily that it may not become fractured.

Declaration: Declare today, I am one of many chosen by Christ.

Action: Study God's Word. Meditate on *John 15:1-17 Jesus Teaches about the Vine and the Branches.*

Prayer: Lord, thank You for choosing me to love, teach, nurture and grow. Help me to tend to the daily care of my branch by staying in Your Word. Continue to remove from me any fruit that appears on my branch that does not meet Your standards. Favor me with producing lasting fruits that I may share and supply with others. In Jesus Name. Amen

Act of Love

But God showed his great love for us by sending Christ to die for us while we were still sinners.
Romans 5:8

This stands out to me. While we were still sinners; while we were still doing wrong; while we were still offending God; while we were still unaccepting of Him - God sacrificed His Son to show His unconditional love for us.

Each time I meditated on this scripture it brought me to tears. Not only did God show His unconditional love but Christ also showed His unconditional love.

Can you remember that as a child you might get the blame for a sibling's act of wrongdoing? You would immediately start declaring – I didn't do it! Why am I getting punished!

Christ never questioned His Father. He never declared – why me? Christ was sinless. He didn't sin. We did! And yet, He was being sacrificed. Not punished but sent to die.

What amazing acts of love shown by the Father and the Son.

If they loved me then; they loved me in the darkest moments of my season.

If I was worthy of their love then; I was worthy of their love when others turned away.

If they accepted me then; they accepted me when I failed in my responsibilities.

God sacrificed His Son as an act of love. Christ died for our sins as an act of love. How can we not love ourselves and others when we have received the ultimate acts of love from God and Christ?

Declaration: Declare today, I am blessed with the unconditional love of God and Christ.

Action: Study God's Word. Meditate daily on this scripture and receive the double blessings of this unconditional love.

Prayer: Lord, thank You for Your unconditional love. In the darkest moments of my season, You loved me. When others turned away, You loved me. When others rejected me, You loved me. Your love is steadfast and true. Help me to love myself and others unconditionally as You and Christ love me. In Jesus Name. Amen

Do You Love Him?

If you love me, obey my commandments
John 14:15

As I anchored myself in God's Word, I came to understand that this scripture is not about the ten commandments received by Moses. It is about the many commandments that Jesus Christ has given us in the New Testament.

The ten commandments I see as do's and don'ts against others. I look upon the commandments of Jesus Christ as teachings on living life as a Christian.

As I anchored myself in God's Word and discovered Christ's commandments, I found guidance to help me through however long my season would be.

Below are just a few of my favorites from what I like to call "The Disciples Handbook".

Repentance - *Matthew 4:17: From then on Jesus began to preach, "Repent of your sins and turn to God, for the Kingdom of Heaven is near."*

Following Christ – *Luke 9:23: Then he said to the crowd, If any of you wants to be my follower, you must give up your own way; take up your cross daily, and follow me.*

Loving Others - *John 15:12: This is my commandment: Love each other in the same way I have loved you.*

Seeking God - *Matthew 6:33: Seek the Kingdom of God above all else, and live righteously, and he will give you everything you need.*

Prayer - *Matthew 6:6: But when you pray, go away by yourself, shut the door behind you, and pray to your Father in private. Then your Father, who sees everything, will reward you.*

Fasting - *Matthew 6:16-17: And when you fast, don't make it obvious, as the hypocrites do, for they try to look miserable and disheveled so people will admire them for their fasting. I tell you the truth, that is the only reward they will ever get. But when you fast, comb your hair and wash your face.*

Forgiveness - *Matthew 18:21-22: Then Peter came to him and asked, "Lord, how often should I forgive someone who sins against me? Seven times?" "No, not seven times," Jesus replied, "but seventy times seven!"*

Communion - *Matthew 26:26-29: As they were eating, Jesus took some bread and blessed it. Then he broke it in pieces and gave it to the disciples, saying, "Take this and eat it, for this is my body." And he took a cup of wine and gave thanks to God for it. He gave it to them and said, "Each of you drink from it, for this is my blood, which confirms the covenant between God and his people. It is poured out as a sacrifice to forgive the sins of many. Mark my words-I will not drink wine again until the day I drink it new with you in my Father's Kingdom."*

If you are worshiping Christ, you should also be following His rules. I encourage you to anchor yourself and study the New Testament. Highlight, underline, and journal the commandments of Christ that speak to you. Look for scriptures that direct you to take action – ask, be, be not, beware, bless, do, do not, follow, give, keep, love, pray, rejoice, seek, submit, take heed.

Declaration: Declare today, I am a Disciple of Christ and strive to obey His commandments.

Action: Study God's Word. Study the *Gospels-Matthew, Mark, Luke, John.*

Prayer: Lord, thank You for Your Word. Thank You for Your teachings to guide me in living my life for You. I love You and I will strive to obey Your commandments. In Jesus Name. Amen

Real Love

This is real love – not that we loved God, but that he loved us and sent his Son as a sacrifice to take away our sins.
1 John 4:10

I grew up on and still love old school music – Motown, the Philadelphia Sound, Rhythm and Blues. One of my favorite songs is Real Love by Mary J Blige. The lyrics go:

Real love
I'm searching for a real love
Someone to set my heart free
Real love
I'm searching for a real love

I am no longer searching and you can stop searching also.

God gave us real love when He sent His one and only Son to die for our sins. Christ showed us real love when He died sinless for our sins.

John 1:18 tell us of the relationship of God and His Son: *No one has ever seen God. But the unique One, who is himself God, is near to the Father's heart. He has revealed God to us.*

God manifested himself into the human form of Jesus Christ allowing us to experience His real love physically.

To see His love through the works of Christ.
To hear His love through the words of Christ.
To feel His love through the touch of Christ.

To taste His love through communion with Christ.
To smell His love through the pleasing aroma of Christ.

Christ's love is real. Christ's love is true. Christ's love set our hearts free as told in *Matthew 27:51*: *At that moment the curtain in the sanctuary of the Temple was torn in two, from top to bottom. The earth shook, rocks split apart.*

Christ showed us real love by dying for our sins and forever removing the barrier between us and God. Setting our hearts free to form personal relationships with God.

Whenever you are feeling unloved, unwanted, unworthy – open God's Word and know that you are loved.

Declaration: Declare today, I have the real love of God and am no longer searching.

Action: Study God's Word. Meditate on scriptures on God's Love. Study *1 John 4:7-21-Loving One Another.*

Prayer: Lord, thank You for Your real, pure, unconditional love. When I am lost, You love me. When I am burdened, You love me. When I am alone, You love me. Your love carries me through. Your love is an anointing upon my life. Through my relationship with Christ, I can see, hear, feel, taste and smell Your unconditional love. In Jesus Name. Amen

Love Challenge

But to you who are willing to listen, I say, love your enemies! Do good to those who hate you. Bless those who curse you. Pray for those who hurt you.

Luke 6:27-28

Every month on social media someone is creating and issuing a challenge – ice bucket challenge, mannequin challenge, cinnamon challenge, etc.

But did you know that Jesus Christ issued the challenge of all challenges – the Love Your Enemies Challenge.

In my season of struggle, I would have failed this challenge. How do I love my enemies? How do I ask a blessing on someone who is hurting me? How do I rise above these feelings to be obedient to Christ?

It was when I re-anchored myself in the Word and walked with Christ in Luke, that my eyes were opened to how Christ loved His enemies.

Jesus was betrayed by Judas and the Disciples were ready to fight. As Jesus was being arrested, Peter sliced off the ear of one of the servants. Jesus stopped him, essentially telling Peter – No. That is not who we are and that is not what we do. Jesus then reached out healed the man with His touch.

So, how do we love our enemies? We follow the example set by Christ. We love like Jesus. We love with compassion, care, friendship, forgiveness. We love with showing goodwill and acts of kindness. *Proverbs 25:21: If your enemies are hungry, give them food to eat. If they are thirsty, give them water to drink. Romans 12:14: Bless those who persecute you. Don't curse them; pray that God will bless them.*

Follow the examples set by Christ.

Declaration: Declare today, I accept Christ's Love Challenge.

Action: Study God's Word. Study the *Book of Luke* and walk with Christ through his life.

Prayer: Lord, I accept Your Love Challenge. Teach me to love my enemies; do good to those who hate me; bless those who curse me; pray for those who hurt me. Open my heart to love others as Christ loved me. In Jesus Name. Amen

Do Everything with Love

And do everything with love.
1 Corinthians 16:14

In the second half of my season, I adopted this scripture to help me get through the day. Do everything with love.

Everything – all things; life in general; current situation. Do everything with love.

I paid my bills with love. I went grocery shopping with love. I worked my job with love. I took my walks with love. I handled workplace hostility with love. I even dealt with my bankruptcy with love. Sounds strange. But it works!

The more I did things with love – I realized how blessed I was.

If I paid a bill – I was blessed with the finances to do so.
If I purchased groceries – I was blessed to have food on the table.
If I worked my job – I was blessed with employment.
If I took my walk – I was blessed with the beauty of God's nature.
If I faced hostility – I was blessed with patience from God.
If I honored my bankruptcy – I was blessed with saving my home.

Proverbs 11:2 tells us: *Pride leads to disgrace, but with humility comes* wisdom. To find the ability to do all things with love we have to let go of our pride and humble ourselves.

Doing everything with love led me to draw closer to God. How? Prayer. I had to go into prayer to let go of my pride and humble myself. I had to go into prayer to gain patience. I had to go into prayer to silence my words. I had to go into prayer to give thanks for the blessings on my life.

Do everything with love. It is hard to do – but it can be done. One day at a time.

Declaration: Declare today, I will do my best to do everything with love. One day at a time.

Action: Study God's Word. Focus on doing one thing each day with love. See God's blessings in your life.

Prayer: Lord, thank You for Your love. Thank You for the daily blessings on my life. As I face each day, open my heart and spirit to do everything with love. Help me to appreciate, enjoy and delight in all things You place in my life. In Jesus Name. Amen

Praise
Let everything that has breath praise the LORD! Praise the LORD!
Psalm 150:6 (ESV)

Prayer
Don't worry about anything; instead, pray about everything. Tell God what you need, and thank him for all he has done.
Philippians 4:6

Worship
Serve the LORD with gladness!
Come into his presence with singing!
Psalm 100:2 (ESV)

Be Grateful

Enter his gates with thanksgiving; go into his courts with praise.
Give thanks to him and praise his name.
Psalm 100:4

One of my favorite gospels is *Be Grateful (Walter Hawkins and the Love Center Choir)*. The song says – "be grateful, even through the hard times and the good times too."

It took me a while to embrace the act of being thankful for challenging times. Then I learned that it is during these times we draw nearer to God. As scripture says:

2 Corinthians 12:9-10 – Each time he said, "My grace is all you need. My power works best in weakness." So now I am glad to boast about my weaknesses, so that the power of Christ can work through me. That's why I take pleasure in my weaknesses, and in the insults, hardships, persecutions, and troubles that I suffer for Christ. For when I am weak, then I am strong.

When we draw nearer to God in our weakness, He becomes stronger and we in turn, become stronger through God's strength.

Give God thanks and praise for the challenges that draw you nearer to Him and make you stronger.

Declaration: Declare today, at my weakest, I am stronger in Christ.

Action: Study God's Word. Meditate on *Psalm 100 His Steadfast Love Endures Forever (ESV)*

Prayer: Lord, I am truly grateful that Your grace is sufficient for me. It is through my challenges, problems, and weaknesses You are made stronger. I draw nearer to You and become stronger through Your strength. In Jesus Name. Amen.

Give God Praise

"Be still and know that I am God!
I will be honored by every nation.
I will be honored throughout the world."
Psalm 46:10

W hen I study on this scripture, it speaks to me in two ways. First as a Child of God to be still and know that He is my Father. Second as a Child of God to know my place and humble myself.

Psalm 100:3 tells us – *Acknowledge that the LORD is God! He made us, and we are his. We are his people, the sheep of his pasture.* He is our creator, our Father. We belong to Him. He is our Shepherd. We are covered with His hedge of protection. He's our rock, our sword, our shield. Be still. Remain calm. Be silent. Understand God is all-powerful over-all nations, heaven and earth. He can and He will fight our battles.

Isaiah 2:17 tells us pride and arrogance of man will not stand. We are children of God – we are NOT God. *Human pride will be humbled, and human arrogance will be brought down.* We will be humbled and the LORD alone will be honored and praised.

Our service in God's Kingdom is to bring Him the Glory. We are to spread the word of the Good News of God's Kingdom, not boast of our works.

Be still and know. Humble yourself in God's Service. Lift Him up – give God the praise!

To God be the Glory!

Declaration: Declare today, to God be the Glory!

Action: Study God's Word. Meditate on scriptures on the Glory of God.

Prayer: Lord, I lift You up and give You praise. Thank You for the many ways in which You are my Father. I still myself and know. I humble myself and serve You. I give You all Glory and Praise! In Jesus Name. Amen

How We Should Pray

*Our Father in heaven, may your name be kept holy. May your
Kingdom come soon. May your will be done on earth, as it is in
heaven. Give us today the food we need, and forgive us our sins, as
we have forgiven those who sin against us. And don't let us yield to
temptation, but rescue us from the evil one.*
Matthew 6:10-13

I was always hesitant to pray out loud because I thought my prayer
had to be loud and long. I had to cover everybody, everything and
every problem. What I call "performance praying" or "praying to be
seen". I had to be on!

Through the first part of my season, there were "just in time" and
"why won't you help me" prayers. In the second part of my season,
as I re-anchored in the Word, I studied and meditated on this
scripture and it changed my prayer life. Jesus himself was teaching
me how to pray - honestly and genuinely.

*"When you pray, don't babble on and on as the Gentiles do. They
think their prayers are answered merely by repeating their words
again and again. Don't be like them, for your Father knows exactly
what you need even before you ask him!" Matthew 6:7-8*

Prayer is part of our relationship with the Father. Prayer is personal.
A conversation between child and parent. Sitting at the feet of our
Father, we can tell Him things we cannot tell anyone else. We can
lay ourselves bare, with no fear of judgement.

Yes, God knew all about my problems. But when I prayed and told
Him of my problems – things shifted.

Prayer creates balance. In *Matthew 11:28*, Jesus tells us: *Come to me, all of you who are weary and carry heavy burdens, and I will give you rest.* The day-to-day, wear and tear of life can be overwhelming – family, work, relationships, finances, health, etc. We can pour out our words to our Father who already knows our needs. Knowing that I can go to my Father at any time, day or night, with any issue – helps eliminate fear and anxiety. The words pour out and peace washes over me.

Prayer provides hope. *God is our refuge and strength, always ready to help in times of trouble. So we will not fear when earthquakes come and the mountains crumble into the sea. Let the oceans roar and foam. Let the mountains tremble as the waters surge! Psalm 46:1-3.* In today's world we are faced with poverty, sickness, financial woes, violence, racial disharmony, rumors of wars. But our Father is forever present. *Lamentations 3:37* tells us - *Who can command things to happen with the Lord's permission?* Nothing happens on this earth without God. He has all authority. He will keep evil away from our doorsteps.

Whether your prayers are long or short, loud or silent, passionate or serene - God is to be honored, respected. He already knows what we need, and He will provide it to us. Honor God. Remain faithful to Him. Give Him the glory.

Activate your prayer life. Pray as Christ instructed us to pray.

Declaration: Declare today, prayer is a spiritual discipline in my life.

Action: Study God's Word. Meditate on *Matthew 6:5-14-Jesus Teaches About Prayer.*

Prayer: Our Father in heaven, may Your name be kept holy. May Your Kingdom come soon. May Your will be done on earth, as it is in heaven. Give me today the food I need, and forgive me my sins, as I have forgiven those who sin against me. And don't let me yield to temptation, but rescue me from the evil one. In Jesus Name. Amen

Stop, Drop, and Pray

*God is our refuge and strength, always ready to help in times of
trouble.*
Psalm 46:1

STOP trying to fix the problem.
DROP to my knees.
PRAY to our Father who is always nearby.

This now is how I deal with any issue that comes my way. Prayer is a spiritual discipline that is key in my life.

God is our Father who provides shelter, protection and safety. He provides us with power, force and might. He is always available. God's protection is not temporary. His protection is not for certain situations. He will aid and assist in all troubles, trials, tribulations, anxieties, and worries.

Pray all the time
1 Thessalonians 5:17 (MSG)

When you stop, drop and pray – you will learn that "trouble don't last always". There is nothing too hard for God.

Declaration: Declare today, I am a Prayer Warrior!

Action: Study God's Word. Stop, drop and pray! Meditate on scriptures on prayer and the importance of prayer.

Prayer: Lord, You are my refuge and strength. In You I have an ever-present God who is ready, willing and able to help in all times of trouble. I stop, drop and pray–seeking You always. Prayer is key in my life. I am a Prayer Warrior! In Jesus Name. Amen

Peace of Christ

And let the peace that comes from Christ rule in your hearts. For as members of one body, you are called to live in peace. And always be thankful.
Colossians 3:15

My season was filled with stress, self-hatred, sadness, rejection, and fear. I felt alone, unloved, angry, shamed, guilty, worthless, lonely, unloved, and a complete failure. Even on good days, I never felt peace.

What is this peace that comes from Christ? The peace that should be ruling my heart? *John 14:27* tells us of the gift Christ left us: *I am leaving you with a gift-peace of mind and heart. And the peace I give is a gift the world cannot give. So, don't be troubled or afraid.*

Throughout my spiritual growth, I have had to learn and continue to learn that accepting Christ does not end my struggles. The struggle is real. Christ gives us the tools to deal with our struggles. One of those tools is peace.

Peace of mind and heart. Peace to know that our troubles do not last forever. Peace to know that whatever life throws our way – conflict, hardship, loss, pain, fear, etc. - God is still on the throne.

And it is God's true peace that Christ gives us when we accept and live in Christ. *Philippians 4:7: Then you will experience God's peace, which exceeds anything we can understand. His peace will guard your hearts and minds as you live in Christ Jesus.*

So, what is the peace that comes from Christ and should rule our heart? It is placing all trust in God. Knowing that God is in control always. That no matter what we may be going through, as a child of God, we have Him standing guard over our hearts. And for that we should be truly grateful.

Accept the gift of peace Christ has given you.

Declaration: Declare today, I have the Peace of Christ.

Action: Study God's Word. Meditate on scriptures on peace.

Prayer: Lord, thank You for the gift of peace. Your peace washes over me and guards my heart. Living with the Peace of Christ helps me to transform – hate to love; sorrow to joy; despair to hope; fear to confidence; conflict to peace. Guide me to share with others the true Peace of Christ which comes from God. In Jesus Name. Amen

Representing Christ

*And whatever you do or say, do it as a representative of the Lord
Jesus, giving thanks through him to God the Father.*
Colossians 3:17

As I re-anchored myself in God's Word, this scripture helped me
to understand what it means to be a representative of Christ.

Accepting Christ means accepting and living His values. Accepting
Christ means accepting and developing His characteristics.
Accepting Christ means representing Him in all we do.

Our representation of Christ cannot be lip service only. Our words
must match our actions.

Are we sharing the same values of Christ?

Service – *For even the Son of Man came not to be served but to serve
others and to give his life as a ransom for many. Matthew 20:28*

Compassion – *They kept demanding an answer, so he stood up again
and said, "All right, but let the one who has never sinned throw the
first stone!" John 8:7*

Peace – *Turn away from evil and do good. Search for peace and
work to maintain it. 1 Peter 3:11*

Thankfulness – *Be thankful in all circumstances, for this is God's
will for you who belong to Christ Jesus. 1 Thessalonians 5:18*

Love – *Jesus replied, "'You must love the LORD your God with all your heart, all your soul, and all your mind.' This is the first and greatest commandment. A second is equally important. 'Love your neighbor as yourself.' Matthew 22:37-39*

Are we working to develop the characteristics of Christ? Are we faithful, prayerful, patient, loving, humble, obedient, giving, virtuous, forgiving?

When we become new in Christ, we begin living a new life. A life that represents Christ.

How do you represent the Lord and Savior?

Declaration: Declare today, I am a representative of Christ. I share the values of Christ and work towards developing the characteristics of Christ.

Action: Study God's Word. Meditate on scriptures on Christ values and characteristics. Meditate on *Colossians 3:1-17-Living the New Life*.

Prayer: Lord, thank You for choosing me to be a representative of You. In all I speak and do, let me do it in Your name. I want to share Your values. I want to develop Your characteristics. Let my actions speak louder than my words. Help me to live a life that represents You. In Jesus Name. Amen

Power of a 6-letter Word

I tell you, you can pray for anything, and if you believe that you've received it, it will be yours.
Mark 11:24

I am fascinated with this 6-letter word that carries so much power.
PRAYER

To understand the power of PRAYER. We must understand the meaning of transformation.

Transformation: an act, process, or instance of <u>transforming</u> or being <u>transformed</u>

We need to understand transformation because we can bend our knee to our Father in prayer and by the time, we rise the transformation has begun and, in some instances completed.

<u>Weakness to strength</u>
I bend my knee to my Father in weakness.

I rise in strength because I know my Father will meet me at my point of weakness and make me strong. *2 Corinthians 12:10: That's why I take pleasure in my weaknesses, and in the insults, hardships, persecutions, and troubles that I suffer for Christ. For when I am weak, then I am strong.*

I rise empowered by His promise. *Isaiah 40:31: But those who trust in the LORD will find new strength. They will soar high on wings like eagles. They will run and not grow weary. They will walk and not faint.*

71

Lost but found

I bend my knee to my Father seeking that connection. *Jeremiah 29:13: If you look for me wholeheartedly, you will find me.*

I rise rejoicing because I have made the connection. *Jeremiah 29:14 – I will be found by you, declares the Lord.*

Warrior for God

I bend my knee to my Father to defend Him against those who work against His Kingdom *Ephesians 6:12: For we are not fighting against flesh-and-blood enemies, but against evil rulers and authorities of the unseen world, against mighty powers in this dark world, and against evil spirits in the heavenly places.*

I rise rejoicing because I have been handed the tools needed to defeat the enemy. *Matthew 16:19: And I will give you the keys of the Kingdom of Heaven. Whatever you forbid on earth will be forbidden in heaven, and whatever you permit on earth will be permitted in heaven.*

I rise rejoicing because I am clothed, armed and ready. *Ephesians 6:11: Put on all of God's armor so that you will be able to stand firm against all strategies of the devil.*

Cleansed of Sins

I bend my knee to my Father in sickness from sin *1 John 1:9: But, if we confess our sins to him, he is faithful and just to forgive us our sins and cleanse us from all wickedness.*

I rise cleansed of all thoughts, acts, iniquities, unclean spirits. *Mark 9:29: Jesus replied, "This kind can be cast out only by prayer.*

United-One Church

I bend my knee to my Father in unity with my fellow Sisters and Brothers. *1 Corinthians 12:27: All of you together are Christ's body, and each of you is a part of it.*

I rise in glory for the body of Christ is the Church. And the Church is a House of Prayer for all nations. *Isaiah 56:7: for my house shall be called a house of prayer for all peoples.*

Utilize the power of Prayer. Pray in faith, pray with belief in your heart. Know before you even pray that your prayer has been answered.

Declaration: Declare today, Prayer is a powerful daily discipline in my life.

Action: Study God's Word. Meditate on scriptures on prayer.

Prayer: Lord thank You for the power of Prayer. Prayer is transforming, cleansing, uniting. I stand on faith that whatever I ask for I have received. I receive it as You would give to me – in Your way, in Your timing, for Your purpose. Your Will be done. In Jesus Name. Amen

Go Bold

So, let us come boldly to the throne of our gracious God. There we will receive his mercy, and we will find grace to help us when we need it most.
Hebrews 4:16

Think back to when you were a child and you needed help. You ran to your parents with your request expecting to receive help.

That is how we are to go to our Father. Boldly! Strong and confident that He will help us.

Prayer is our personal communication tool with our Father. In trust we can go to the throne of God in prayer so that we may receive His mercy and grace.

Do not be shy. Do not be timid. He is our Father, who already knows what we need – so go BOLDLY to our Father – STRONG and CONFIDENT.

Start praying boldly.

Declaration: Declare today, I will go boldly to God in prayer.

Action: Study God's Word. Meditate on *Psalm 86:1-Bend down, O, LORD, and hear my prayer; answer me, for I need your help.*

Prayer: Lord, I come to You boldly in prayer. You are a merciful and gracious Father. Thank You for always helping me in my time of need. In Jesus Name. Amen

Power of the 23rd

The LORD is my shepherd; I shall not want. He makes me lie down in green pastures. He leads me beside still waters. He restores my soul. He leads me in paths of righteousness for His name's sake. Even though I walk through the valley of the shadow of death, I will fear no evil, for you are with me; your rod and your staff, they comfort me. You prepare a table before me in the presence of my enemies; You anoint my head with oil; my cup overflows. Surely goodness and mercy shall follow me all the days of my life. And I shall dwell in the house of the LORD forever.
Psalm 23 (ESV)

The 23rd Psalm comes with God doing so many things for us. And the Psalm serving so many purposes.

It is ***prayer*** in our hour of need; ***declaration of faith*** to announce our trust in God; ***victory statement*** when we face our adversaries.

It is the answer to – Why? – why I serve the Lord; why I honor Him; why I praise Him; why I thank Him; why I love Him.

So, it is written and I receive it…………….

He supplies my every need.
He makes me comfortable.
He guides me to quiet peace.
He lifts my spirit.
He is guiding me into a way of life free from guilt or sin, all with His name in purpose.
In the darkest hours He is with me
giving me strength, hope, easing my grief and trouble.

He shows my enemies I am blessed and protected.
He has anointed me and I am filled with the Spirit beyond its limits.
Without a doubt righteousness and blessings are with me always.
And I will remain in His house forever.

Declaration: Declare today, I believe and receive the 23rd Psalm. The Lord is my shepherd; I shall not want.

Action: Study God's Word. Meditate on the *23rd Psalm*.

Prayer: Lord, thank You for being my Shepherd. Lord, You are my supplier, my comfort, my peace, my lifter, my guide, my light, my strength, my hope. I am blessed, protected and anointed. Thank You for the Psalm of David, my prayer in my hour of need; my declaration of faith; my victory statement to my enemies. In You I have all things. In Jesus Name. Amen

Promises of God

For I know the plans I have for you, says the LORD.
They are plans for good and not for disaster, to give you
a future and a hope.
Jeremiah 29:11

Promise: He Will Help You

Commit everything you do to the LORD.
Trust him, and he will help you.
Psalm 37:5

This is both an <u>Action</u> and <u>Promise</u> scripture. Commitment brings reward. Be obedient and God will do as He promises.

It is difficult to release and let go. Human nature leads us to want to be in control of all things. We tend to think we know what's best and can do what's best. This leads us to have knee-jerk reactions and make poor decisions.

Committing everything to God, our ways and our work, is an act of obedience. That act of obedience is rewarded with God's Promises to act and establish plans for us.

Commit your actions to the LORD, and your plans will succeed.
Proverbs 16:3

Commit ALL THINGS – life, family, job, health, finances, education, service, etc. to God. Live your life as a representative of Christ; nurture your family with the Word of God; perform your job responsibilities as if working for Christ; care for your body and mind as the temple it is for the Holy Spirit; tithe and work faithfully for the advancement of God's Kingdom; educate yourself in God's Word; serve your fellow man with acts of kindness.

Commit everything – Trust Him – Receive His blessings.

Declaration: Declare today, I commit all things in my life to God. I trust Him completely.

Action: Study God's Word. Trust in God completely. Meditate on *Psalm 37 He Will Not Forsake His Saints (ESV)*.

Prayer: Lord, I stand on Your promise to help me. I trust You with everything in my life. I release and let go. Have Your way Lord in all areas of my life – family, job, health, finances, worship. I submit all to Your control and guidance. In Jesus Name. Amen

Promise: He Will Give You Your Heart's Desires

Take delight in the LORD, and he will give you your heart's desires.
Psalm 37:4

This is both an Action and Promise scripture. Get busy delighting yourself in God and get rewarded with His promises.

Delighting yourself in the Lord can be done in many ways – prayer, service, study, teaching, ministering, praise and worship.

One of my favorite ways to delight in God is through music. My praise-list is my everlasting joy. The "fire in my bones" gospel of my Mom's day – brings me joy in times of trouble. The soulful sounds of Aretha Franklin and James Cleveland brings me joy when dealing with anxiety. The pop of Walter Hawkins and the Love Center Choir gets my praise dance going and the joy overflowing. The quiet praise of Psalmist Raine and Refresh brings me a calm joy for prayer.

Isaiah 58:14 tells us of the promises of God when we delight in the Lord – *Then the LORD will be your delight. I will give you great honor and satisfy you with the inheritance I promised to your ancestor Jacob. I, the LORD, have spoken!* Do you see God's Promises? God rewards our glorifying Him by honoring us. When we honor and respect God – He in turn honors and respects us.

He identifies us as the heirs of Jacob and promises to feed us our inheritance as promised to Jacob in *Genesis 28:13-15 – At the top of the stairway stood the LORD, and he said, "I am the LORD, the God of your grandfather Abraham, and the God of your father, Isaac.*

The ground you are lying on belongs to you. I am giving it to you and your descendants. Your descendants will be as numerous as the dust of the earth! They will spread out in all directions-to the west and the east, to the north and the south. And all the families of the earth will be blessed through you and your descendants. What's more, I am with you, and I will protect you wherever you go. One day I will bring you back to this land. I will not leave you until I have finished giving you everything I have promised you."

We are the descendants of Jacob. We are in the north, south, east and west. The blessings of Abraham, Isaac, and Jacob flow down our family lines to our descendants.

Build your personal relationship with God. Grow closer in knowing Him. In whatever way you choose to take delight in God – do it!

Declaration: Declare today, along with prayer, praise and worship, I will delight myself in the Lord in ways that are unique to me.

Action: Study God's Word. Meditate on *Psalm 37 He Will Not Forsake His Saints (ESV)*.

Prayer: Lord, I stand on Your promise to fulfill my heart's desires. I honor and respect You with my praise. You are Lord, God of my ancestors, Abraham, Isaac and Jacob. Thank You, Father, for the blessings that flows down to me and my descendants. In Jesus Name. Amen

Promise: The Holy Spirit

And I will ask the Father, and he will give you another Advocate,
who will never leave you. He is the Holy Spirit, who leads into all
truth. The world cannot receive him, because it isn't looking for
him and doesn't recognize him. But you know him because he lives
with you now and later will be in you.
John 14:16-17

Knowing that He will be leaving us, Jesus is standing in the gap and asking on our behalf for God the Father to send us another Advocate that will never leave us.

"Another" – Jesus was our first advocate. Our first champion, supporter, patron, helper, counselor, teacher. He knows we cannot survive without help from another Advocate. An Advocate that will never leave us – the Holy Spirit. The Holy Spirit is a powerful entity that we who have sought Christ and accepted Christ will receive.

Jesus tells us in *John 16:13* the Holy Spirit is the Spirit of truth: *When the Spirit of truth comes, he will guide you into all truth. He will not speak on his own but will tell you what he has heard. He will tell you about the future.* The truth we receive from the Holy Spirit will be directly from the Father. We will learn "all truth" – our learning does not end with the death of Christ.

Jesus tells us in *John 14:26* that the Holy Spirit is also our teacher: *But when the Father sends the Advocate as my representative – that is, the Holy Spirit – he will teach you everything and will remind you of everything I have told you.* Not only will we continue to learn from the Holy Spirit but the Spirit will not let us forget the teachings of Christ. As we study God's Word, the Spirit will open our eyes to see and our ears to hear what Christ is speaking to us through His teachings.

Those who do not know Christ cannot receive the Holy Spirit. Because they do not believe they cannot know the Holy Spirit. We who believe are blessed because we know Christ walked among us in flesh and will now be within us in the Holy Spirit.

Our Father has given us His Son and is now giving us His Holy Spirit. We are God's Children joined to him by the Holy Spirit. *Romans 8:15-16: So you have not received a spirit that makes you fearful slaves. Instead, you received God's Spirit when he adopted you as his own children. Now we call him, "Abba, Father." For his Spirit joins with our spirit to affirm that we are God's children.*

Read that again! You received God's Spirit when He adopted YOU as His own child. He is Abba, Father!

Declaration: Declare today, I am a daughter/son of God. I am joined to His Sprit by Christ and the Holy Spirit

Action: Study God's Word. Meditate on *Galatians 5:22-23-Fruits of the Holy Spirit*

Prayer: Lord, I stand on Your promise of the Holy Spirit. Father, open my heart, mind, and soul to receive the Holy Spirit and His truth. Cleanse me Holy Spirit and teach me everything I need to know to live a new life in Christ. In Jesus Name. Amen

Promise: He Will Come Close to You

So humble yourselves before God. Resist the devil, and he will flee from you. Come close to God, and God will come close to you. Wash your hands you sinners; purify your hearts, for your loyalty is divided between God and the world.
James 4:7-8

This is both an <u>Action</u> and <u>Promise</u> scripture. Get close to God and He will get close to you.

We cannot be loyal to both God and the ways of the world. Serving God does not work like that.

Our Father is a jealous Father and wants our loyalty. *Exodus 34:14* tells us: *You must worship no other gods, for the LORD, whose very name is Jealous, is a God who is jealous about His relationship with you.*

We cannot ignore Him, Monday through Saturday to spend time in the world; then acknowledge Him on Sunday. He is not a part-time Father. He does not have shared custody with the world. He is our primary caregiver with full custody.

How do we get close to God?

1. Humble ourselves before God: let go of our prideful ways; give ourselves over to God's will.
2. Resist the devil: send the enemy packing; use scripture as Jesus did to fight off the devil.
3. Come close to God: submit our lives to God; study His Word; build a relationship with God.

4. Wash our hands and purify our hearts: cleanse ourselves of our sinful nature; accept Christ and seek to live a pure life prayer, worship, service, love.

You have to take the first step! Get close to God and He will get close to you.

Declaration: Declare today, I resist the devil and pledge my loyalty to God.

Action: Study God's Word. Meditate on scriptures on drawing nearer to God.

Prayer: Lord, I stand on Your promise to come close to me. I commit myself to You and pledge my loyalty. I have no other gods before You. Father, help me to let go of my prideful ways. Holy Spirit lead me to scripture to help fight off the devil. Cleanse me Father and help me to live a pure life of prayer, worship, service and love. In Jesus Name. Amen

Promise: Strength, Help, Support

Don't be afraid, for I am with you.
Don't be discouraged, for I am your God.
I will strengthen you and help you.
I will hold you up with my victorious right hand.
Isaiah 41:10

This is an <u>Action</u>, <u>Promise</u> and <u>Acknowledgement</u> scripture.

Action: <u>do not</u> be afraid; <u>do not</u> be discouraged.

Promise: strength, help, support

Acknowledgement: I am. I am. I will. I will.

Close your eyes and imagine the conversation with our Father:

Me: Father, I'm scared.
Father: Don't be afraid. I'm with you always.

Me: Father, I'm discouraged.
Father: Don't be discouraged. You are my child. I am your Father.

Father: I am always going to be here for you my daughter. I will strengthen you where you are weak and help you at all times. I am but a thought and a whisper away. You can always call on me. As Moses told Joshua in *Deuteronomy 31:8*: *Do not be afraid or discouraged, for the LORD will personally go ahead of you. He will be with you; he will neither fail you nor abandon you.* As I did with Joshua and my children in Israel, I personally go ahead of you each day. I am a God of Victory which means you are a Child of Victory.

I will catch you when you stumble, pick you up when you fall and carry you when you feel as if you cannot take another step.

What shall we say about such wonderful things as these?
If God is for us, who can ever be against us?
Romans 8:31

Strength, help, support. There is no match for our Father's love.

Declaration: Declare today, I am a Child of Victory.

Action: Study God's Word. Meditate on *Romans 8:31-39 Nothing Can Separate Us from God's Love.*

Prayer: Lord, I stand on Your promises of strength, help, and support. You are not a God to lie or deceive. As You were with my ancestors, You are with me. I call on Your name at all times. There is no match for Your love. In Jesus Name. Amen

Promise: Salvation

If you openly declare that Jesus is Lord and believe in your heart that God raised him from the dead, you will be saved.
Romans 10:9

This is an <u>Action</u> and <u>Promise</u> scripture. Declare. Believe. Receive. How simple is that?

If you are seeking soul salvation - open your mouth, where all may hear, and declare that Jesus Christ is the LORD and Savior. Believe in your heart that our Father did indeed raise him from the dead. Save your soul from the sins of the world.

Jesus promises us in *Matthew 10:32 – "Everyone who acknowledges me publicly here on earth, I will also acknowledge before my Father in heaven."*

It means nothing to acknowledge Christ in private. Our declaration must be made publicly, whenever the opportunity presents itself, so that it is known our LORD and Savior was raised from the dead and our salvation comes from Him.

Close your eyes and visualize. You are standing before the throne. Christ is sitting at the right hand of God. Christ speaks - 'Father, this is your child'.

Jesus goes above and beyond, enhancing the promise of salvation with the promise of an eternal reward: *All who are victorious will be clothed in white. I will never erase their names from the Book of Life, but I will announce before my Father and his angels that they are mine. Revelations 3:5*

What amazing promises and rewards from such a simple action. Declare and believe - salvation is received; clothed in white; entered into the Book of Life; announced before God and his angels.

Declaration: Declare today, Jesus is Lord

Action: Study God's Word. Meditate on *Romans 10:5-21 Salvation is for Everyone*

Prayer: Lord I stand on Your promise of salvation. As You acknowledge me before our Father, I publicly acknowledge You here on earth. I openly declare that Jesus is Lord. Lord, thank You for my salvation that comes from You. In Jesus Name. Amen

Promise: God's Word is Forever

The grass withers and the flowers fade, but the word of our God stands forever.
Isaiah 40:8

Throughout my season, I would talk through a problem with others only to receive opinions that changed constantly, were given with no clarity and included falsehoods.

When I re-anchored myself, I relearned a valuable truth – God's Word is always. It never changes. It has no hidden agendas. It is true. It is steady. It is constant.

Peter quotes Isaiah and reminds us of God's Word being forever in *1 Peter 1:24-25: As the Scriptures say, "People are like grass; their beauty is like a flower in the field. The grass withers and the flower fades. But the word of the Lord remains forever."*

All things in our life will eventually go away – family, friends, careers, homes, all material things. But God's Word is always. It is as God is – the same yesterday, today and tomorrow. It stands forever.

When a problem arises now, my first conversation is with God. *Psalm 119:105* tells us God's Word is the solution to our problems and needs. *Your word is a lamp to guide my feet and a light for my path.* The Word of God gives us direction to the right path. His Word lights our way when we encounter darkness on that path.

Jesus told us - *Heaven and earth will disappear, but my words will never disappear. Luke 21:33*

Drop you anchor in God's Word. Let it draw you in. Let it teach you. Let it challenge you. Seek out scriptures that will guide you and help you on your path. Let God's Word make you question the way of the world.

Declaration: Declare today, God's Word is forever.

Action: Study God's Word. Meditate on *Psalm 119 Your Word Is a Lamp to My Feet (ESV)*.

Prayer: Lord I stand on Your Word forever. Thank You for Your Word. Your Word is my anchor. Open my eyes to see; my ears to hear; my heart mind and soul to receive. Father, I pray Your Word draws me in, teaches me, challenges me, makes me think. Your Word is forever. In Jesus Name. Amen

Promise: Rest

*Then Jesus said, Come to me, all of you who are weary and carry
heavy burdens, and I will give you rest
Matthew 11:28*

The first part of my season was loaded with heavy burdens. I was weighed down from the moment I woke each morning until I went to sleep at night. Rinse and repeat every day.

The second part of my season, I dropped anchor in God's Word and ran to Christ. I heeded His word and laid my troubles at His feet.

Christ's rest is not your normal rest. It is comforting, healing, refreshing.

God is not saying stop your work. The struggle is real. God is saying – Yes, it is real, it is hard, but I am here. I will comfort you, start the healing, refresh your spirit and recover your strength.

Rest in Christ brings you – renewal, refreshening, restoration, recovering, and healing.

Declaration: Declare today, in Christ I find my rest.

Action: Study God's Word. Meditate on *Matthew 11:20-30-Jesus Promises Rest for the Soul*

Prayer: Lord, I stand on Your promise of rest. Father, I may come to You weary and heavily burdened, but rest in You is – renewing, refreshening, restoring, recovering, and healing. The rest I receive from You is filled with love and peace. Father, I sit at Your feet resting in thankfulness that You Lord are the well of living water I drink from each day. In Jesus Name. Amen

Promise: Renewal

But those who trust in the LORD will find new strength. They will soar high on wings like eagles. They will run and not grow weary. They will walk and not faint.
Isaiah 40:31

This is an <u>Action</u> and <u>Promise</u> scripture.

Wait and trust.

Waiting is difficult but the Promises of God from this scripture are amazing: renewal, strength, ability to soar, restoration, revival, power, energy.

When we wait on the Lord, we are not standing in line. We are trusting and believing in His Word. We are getting out of His way and letting Him work. Waiting builds our trust; strengthens our faith and teaches us patience.

2 Corinthians 4:8-9 says it best: *We are pressed on every side by troubles, but we are not crushed. We are perplexed, but not driven to despair. We are hunted down, but never abandoned by God. We get knocked down, but we are not destroyed.*

I now wait on the Lord. I do not go until I know I have heard from the Lord.

Wait and trust in the LORD.

Declaration: Declare today, I am not crushed or destroyed. I have renewed strength through Christ. I can soar like the eagles.

Action: Study God's Word. Meditate on *Isaiah 40:12-31-The LORD has no equal*.

Prayer: Lord, I stand on Your promise of Renewal. I wait and place my trust in You. In You I have new strength. I can fly like an eagle. I can run and never get tired. I can walk and do not faint. Life may come at me but hope is never lost. In Jesus Name. Amen

Salvation

*I wait quietly before God,
for my victory comes from him.
Psalm 62:1*

Bear the Cross

The message of the cross is foolish to those who are headed for destruction! But we who are being saved know it is the very power of God.
1 Corinthians 1:18

The song says: *Must Jesus bear the cross alone and all this world go free? No, there's a cross for everyone and there's a cross for me. Thomas Shepherd (1665-1739).*

The *word of the cross* is Jesus dying for our sins. With the death of Jesus, we were delivered from our sins. Those who do not believe in Christ view His death as foolishness. As believers in Christ, we know His death was all powerful!

The cross Christ bore, carried the sins of the world. One can only imagine the weight felt on His body as He endured the taunting and beatings carrying that heavy cross to His death. And lest we forget, Christ was sinless!

Jesus tells us in *Matthew 16:24: If any of you wants to be my follower, you must give up your own way, take up your cross, and follow me.*

What does it mean to take up our cross? We have our own cross to bear. We carry our sins. And the cross we carry must lead us to death. The death of our former selves. We must let go of our life in order to follow Christ. Following Christ is a true commitment. We will lose family and friends, be taunted and criticized. But the reward of following Christ is worth the pain of the cross.

We must bear our cross so that we may be free! Take up your cross and follow Christ. Let go of your old life.

Declaration: Declare today, I deny myself and take up my cross to follow Christ.

Action: Study God's Word. Meditate on *Matthew 16:24-28-Take Up Your Cross and Follow Jesus (ESV)*.

Prayer: Lord, thank You for carrying the cross and dying for my sins. Your death was all powerful in the name of God. I now take up my cross and follow You. I leave behind my former life and commit myself to Your ways. Strengthen me Lord to follow You and not this world. In Jesus Name. Amen

.

Raised Up

And God will raise us from the dead by his power,
just as he raised our Lord from the dead.
1 Corinthians 6:14

At the lowest point in my season, when I had suicidal thoughts –
God met me and raised me up. Using my mother as His vessel – I
was instructed to end my drifting and re-anchor myself in His Word.

God raised me up from near death when I lost my way. *Acts 2:24*
tells us death could not hold Jesus – *But God released him from the*
horrors of death and raised him back to life, for death could not keep
him in its grip. Death could not hold Jesus and the enemy could not
hold me.

Someday we too will face and conquer death. For now, we must
conquer spiritual death. When we reach a point of not knowing
where to turn or who to go to – Christ is our way.

God will raise us up from death as He did Jesus.

Declaration: Declare today, God has raised me from the dead.

Action: Study God's Word. Anchor yourself in God's Word and
prayer.

Prayer: Lord, thank You for rescuing me when I was at my lowest.
The helmet of salvation calmed my troubled mind. Thank You for
Your saving grace. Lord, You raised me from spiritual death. In You
I was raised from death. Keep me in Your care. In Jesus Name.
Amen

Sin Cannot be Hidden

*Finally, I confessed all my sins to you and stopped trying to hide
my guilt. I said to myself, "I will confess my rebellion to the
LORD." And you forgave me! All my guilt is gone.*
Psalm 32:5

God knows and sees all. It is foolish to lie and deny. *1 John 1:8*
tells us – *If we say we have no sin, we deceive ourselves, and the
truth is not in us.*

Ask yourself as Job did – *"Have I tried to hide my sins like other
people do, concealing my guilt in my heart?" (Job 31:33)* You
cannot deceive God. Job understood this and did not try. In his final
appeal, Job declared that he never hid his sins from God. Can you
make that declaration? It is not too late.

1 John 1:9 tells us – *But if we confess our sins to him, he is faithful
and just to forgive us our sins and to cleanse us from all wickedness.*
Stand today on God's Word. Confess your sin and receive God's
forgiveness.

1 John 1:10 tells us – *If we claim we have not sinned, we are calling
God a liar and showing that his word has no place in our hearts.*
We must understand that to deny our sin verbally or non-verbally is
to bring shame to God.

Do you want to go on record as calling God a liar? I don't!

Declaration: Declare today, I stand today on God's Word. I confess
my sin to receive God's forgiveness.

Action: Study God's Word. Meditate on *1 John 1:5-10-Living in the Light.*

Prayer: Lord, I am a sinner. I confess my sins to You and seek Your forgiveness. In Jesus Name. Amen

In Jesus Name

You haven't done this before. Ask, using my name, and you will receive, and you will have abundant joy.
John 16:24

M*atthew 27:51* tells us that Jesus death has given us a direct connection to God.

At that moment the curtain in the sanctuary of the Temple was torn in two, from top to bottom. The earth shook, rocks split apart.
Matthew 27:51

The barrier that separated humanity from God is gone. We can now draw near to God and be in His presence. It is through Christ we are acceptable to God. However, in order to ask for anything in Jesus name, we have to have a personal relationship with Him.

Jesus told him, "I am the way, the truth, and the life. No one can come to the Father except through me.
John 14:6

You can ask for anything in Jesus name and it will be given. But you must first accept, commit and submit to Christ.

Declaration: Declare today, I accept, commit and submit to Christ.

Action: Study God's Word. Meditate on *John 16 Jesus Teaches about the Holy Spirit and Using His Name in Prayer.*

Prayer: Lord, I accept, commit and submit to You. In Your name, I ask and receive, joy and peace. Touch my heart, mind and soul that

I may remain in Your presence. In Jesus Name. Amen

The Ultimate Goal

The one thing I ask of the LORD – the thing I seek most is to live in the house of the LORD all the days of my life, delighting in the LORD's perfections and meditating in his Temple.
Psalm 27:4

My ultimate goal is to live in my Father's house, be in His presence and to learn at His feet forever.

I see myself in God's Kingdom. Splendidly clothed in a dazzling, flowing white robe, trimmed in purple and gold. Walking the streets of gold, heading to the Holy Temple. I walk through the gates. The air is electric. The atmosphere is changing. I am in His Presence! Pour into me Father.

I declare *Psalm 26:8 – I love your sanctuary, LORD, the place where your glorious presence dwells*. I want to move into my Father's house. Don't you?

And in *John 14:6*, Jesus himself tells us how to seek after and accomplish that goal – *Jesus told him, I am the way, the truth, and the life. No one can come to the Father except through me.*

The way to get to Father's house is simple – a personal relationship with Jesus Christ!

Accept and commit to Christ as your Lord and Savior. Study God's Word. Stay prayerful. Serve in God's Kingdom here on earth. Tithe faithfully to advance God's Kingdom.

Declaration: Declare today, I will live in the house of my Lord all the days of my life.

Action: Study God's Word. Speak over your life Psalm 23:6 – *Surely your goodness and unfailing love will pursue me all the days of my life, and I will live in the house of the LORD forever.*

Prayer: Lord, thank You for having a personal relationship with me. I declare in Jesus name: I will live in Your house. I will look upon Your face and be in Your Holy Presence. To sit at Your feet and bask in Your Glory is my ultimate goal. I accept and commit to You as my Lord and Savior. In Jesus Name. Amen

Repentance, Baptism, Receivership

Now repent of your sins and turn to God,
so that your sins may be wiped away.
Acts 3:19

This is an <u>Action</u> and <u>Promise</u> scripture.

When we denounce our sins and confess our wrongs, God promises our sins will be erased, wiped out.

We can't just denounce our sins and confess – we have to turn away from our sins and not return to them.

In today's world that is difficult. Not everyone will be on board with your new life and your walk with Christ. Each day we are bombarded with opportunities to sin and turn away from God. Giving up vices and breaking old habits sometimes requires ending friendships/relationships. It is hard but necessary for the salvation we seek comes from a relationship with Christ.

Peter tells us in *Acts 2:38: "Each of you must repent of your sins and turn to God, and be baptized in the name of Jesus Christ for the forgiveness of your sins. Then you will receive the gift of the Holy Spirit."* We cannot live a life for Christ without repenting of our sins.

When Christ died for our sins His death removed the barrier between us and God. In repenting our sins, we acknowledge Christ's sinless death and we start to build our personal relationship with God.

Repentance, baptism, receivership.

Declaration: Declare today, I acknowledge the sinless death of my Lord and Savior Jesus Christ and I repent of my sins and turn to God.

Action: Study God's Word. Meditate on scriptures on repentance.

Prayer: Lord, I acknowledge the sinless death You died for me. Strengthen me each day to reject sin and turn away from old habits. Lord, I seek salvation from my relationship with You. Free me from any friendships or relationships that may harm my relationship with You. In Jesus Name. Amen

New Life

This means that anyone who belongs to Christ has become a new person. The old life is gone; a new life has begun!
2 Corinthians 5:17

New life in Christ. Total transformation.

We are not turning over a new leaf. We are re-created on the inside.

We are with Christ and in Christ. New thoughts. New actions. New words. New works, New attitude.

We do not do the things we did in the past. We do not walk or talk as we used to.

We are Champions for Christ. God's Ambassadors. Guardians of Faith

Declaration: Declare today, I have a new life in Christ. I am an Ambassador for God.

Action: Study God's Word. Meditate on *2 Corinthians 5:11-21-We Are God's Ambassadors*

Prayer: Lord, thank You for transforming me and leading me into a new life. Lord, I am not what I want to be. But I am not what I used to be. Lord, continue to break me down and rebuild me. I still have more change and growth ahead of me. Keep me Father on the path to spiritual maturity. In Jesus Name. Amen

Meditate on God's Word

Study this Book of Instruction continually. Meditate on it day and night so you will be sure to obey everything written in it. Only then will you prosper and succeed in all you do.
Joshua 1:8

Notice the scripture states "study" – not read.

The Bible is not a novel. For me, it is a living Book of Life. I call it living because each time I study God's Word, I come away with new knowledge and understanding. I can read a scripture one day and have a clear understanding. Then I can read that same scripture another day and receive a different understanding.

When I would have different understandings of one scripture, it confused me. Until I studied on *2 Timothy 3:16*.

2 Timothy 3:16 tells us – *All Scripture is inspired by god and is useful to teach us what is true and to make us realize what is wrong in our lives. It corrects us when we are wrong and teaches us to do what is right.*

I believe God knows what I need when I start study on a scripture. And He provides the proper instruction that is required.

God's Word is critical in the salvation we receive. Knowing God's Word is the framework of staying on the right path.

Dedicate time to go deep into God's Word. Meditate on God's Word. Stay in God's Word. Be mindful to obey God's Word. Then we will be successful in God's eyes.

Declaration: Declare today, God's Word is my Book of Life.

Action: Study God's Word. Meditate on *2 Timothy 3:16*.

Prayer: Lord, thank You for Your Word. Your Word is my Book of Life. It teaches me what is true. It shows me what is wrong in my life. It corrects me when I am wrong and teaches me to do what is right. Your Word keeps me on the right path. It feeds me when I am hungry and quenches my thirst for knowledge of You. Your Word keeps me anchored and grounded. In Jesus Name. Amen

Jesus Saves

For the Son of Man came to seek and save those who are lost.
Luke 19:10

When I drifted away from Christ, I also suffered what I call "scripture memory loss". Not only did I not have an understanding of scripture, I could not remember scripture.

I did not remember that Christ did not come to condemn me – He came to save me.

I looked upon my failure to make the right decisions during my struggle as an afront to God. I felt I had displeased God by making wrong choices and ending up in a season of struggle. I compounded my mistake by not praying to Him for guidance and drifting away from Him.

But God was not displeased with me – Christ was still seeking me. How do I know this? My feeling of guilt for drifting away. My feeling of knowing there was someone I could turn to. My feeling of thinking I had hurt God.

He was right there and all I had to do was seek Him as He sought me.

Jesus came to save those who were lost. I was one of them.

Declaration: Declare today, I was lost. Jesus saved me.

Action: Study God's Word. Meditate on scriptures on Salvation.

Prayer: Lord, thank You for not giving up on me. Thank You for the guilt I felt when I drifted away. Thank You for seeking me out and saving me. I was lost but now I am found. Saved by Your grace. In Jesus Name. Amen

No Hunger. No Thirst.

Jesus replied,
"I am the bread of life. Whoever comes to me will never be hungry
again. Whoever believes in me will never be thirsty."
John 6:35

Christ is the bread that feeds us. *John 6:48 – Yes, I am the bread of life!*

He is the living water that quenches our thirst. *John 4:14 – But those who drink the water I give will never be thirsty again. It becomes a fresh, bubbling spring within them, giving them eternal life.*

When we receive salvation – we will never hunger or thirst. However, we will be tempted by those who do not seek or have received salvation. When that happens, we can follow the example of Christ and fight that temptation with God's Word.

Matthew 4:1-4: Then Jesus was led by the Spirit into the wilderness to be tempted there by the devil. For forty days and forty nights he fasted and became very hungry. During that time the devil came and said to him, "If you are the Son of God, tell these stones to become loaves of bread." But Jesus told him. "No! The Scriptures say, 'People do not live by bread alone, but by every word that comes from the mouth of God.'"

We must build our relationship with Christ for our spiritual life.

Declaration: Declare today, Christ is the bread that feeds me and the living water that quenches my thirst.

Action: Study God's Word. Meditate on *John 6:22-40 Jesus is the True Bread from Heaven.*

Prayer: Lord, feed me until I want no more. You are the bread of life and the living water. In You I am fed and refreshed. I want a personal relationship with You that grows and thrives every day of my life. In Jesus Name. Amen

Always There

My victory and honor come from God alone. He is my refuge, a
rock where no enemy can reach me.
Psalm 62:7

When I think of God as my rock and my refuge, I think of the ultimate safe room built on an indestructible foundation. It is a permanent room of safety and peace. There is nothing that can destroy the foundation and there is nothing that can penetrate the door and walls to bring me harm. I am protected.

Psalm 46:1 tells us that *God is our refuge and strength, always ready to help in times of trouble.* Study on that! He is not just ready – but **always ready** – always there and always ready.

Always there. Always ready.
I close my eyes and I see Your face.
I open my ears and I hear Your voice.
I sniff and I smell the sweet aroma of Your grace and mercy.
I lift my hand and feel the power of Your mighty touch.
I give You my heart and feel Your love.
I sit at Your feet and feel joy in Your presence.
Always there. Always ready.

Declaration: Declare today, I give God all honor and praise. He is the foundation on which my faith is built. He is always there and always present in my life.

Action: Study God's Word. Meditate on *Psalm 46-God Is Our Fortress (ESV)*.

116

Prayer: Lord, thank You for being my ever-present help in times of trouble. Lord You are my rock. I come to You on bended knee with thankfulness in my heart. You alone are my ultimate safe room. Your love overflows to me in so many ways. You are always present, always here, always comforting, always near. In Jesus Name. Amen

Strength

The LORD is my light and my salvation; whom shall I fear? The LORD is the stronghold of my life; of whom shall I be afraid?
Psalm 27:1 (ESV)

Go to the Rock

Let all that I am wait quietly before God, for my hope is in him. He alone is my rock and my salvation, my fortress where I will not be shaken.
Psalm 62:5-6

One of my favorite hymns is *I Go to The Rock (Dottie Rambo).*

Where do I go when there's nobody else to turn to?
Who do I talk to when nobody wants to listen?
Who do I lean on when there's no foundation stable?

I go to the rock
I know he's able
I go to the rock

When situations arise in my life, I have learned to sit tight in prayerful silence and Go to the Rock. At the Rock I can rest in His strength knowing that I will not be weakened but receive strength.

God is ALL - hope, foundation, salvation, protection.

God is our hope. In Him we can have great expectation of His promises.

God is the foundation on which our faith rests. Not man, not material things, not idolatry.

God is our salvation. Our deliverer. He has delivered us from sin.

God is our protection. Our stronghold against all attacks. With God's protection, nothing can weaken, harm or damage us.

Declaration: Declare today, on Christ the solid rock I stand.

Action: Study God's Word. Meditate on *Psalm 62 My Soul Waits for God Alone (ESV)*.

Prayer: Lord, I give You praise. You alone are my rock, my salvation, my protector. My soul waits in prayerful silence and great expectation of Your Promises. Resting in my faith I receive Your strength and cannot be weakened. You are my all. You are my Rock. On Christ the solid rock I stand. In Jesus Name. Amen

Seek His Face

The LORD says, "I will guide you along the best pathway for your life. I will advise you and watch over you.
Psalm 32:8

$$\mathcal{\longleftarrow}\!\!\mathcal{O}\!\!\mathcal{\longrightarrow}$$

What better teacher than God? What better textbook than His Word?

I call this a "Stress Reliever" scripture. To know that we are under the watchful eye of our Lord and Savior. To know that His counsel is always at hand. To know our Lord and Savior will direct us and teach us the way we should go.

As scripture tells us – *Search for the LORD and for his strength; continually seek him. Psalm 105:4*

In all things, each and every day, no matter the situation – we can seek the Lord – His advice, His guidance, His counsel, His favor, His power, His strength. The list is endless of what God can provide. As God has His eye upon us – we must stay focused on God through study of the Word, daily prayer, attitude of service, praise and worship.

Declaration: Declare today, in all situations in my life, I seek His face.

Action: Study God's Word. Meditate on scriptures on being in God's presence.

Prayer: Lord, You are my teacher, my mentor, my instructor, my guide, my counsel. I shall seek Your face always in all situations. Thank You Father for Your direction in the path I should choose to follow; the manner in which to live my life as Your child. Father God, I stand on Your promises. In Jesus Name. Amen

It's Okay to Be Weak

Each time he said, "My grace is all you need. My power works best in weakness." So now I am glad to boast about my weaknesses, so that the power of Christ can work through me.
2 Corinthians 12:9

Go ahead and shout it out – I am weak!

God's power is strengthened when you admit your weaknesses. He will meet you at your points of weakness and make you strong.

When I look back on my season, I can see where God made me stronger when I was at my weakest. If I knew then, what I know now – I would have shouted at the top of my lungs – I AM WEAK!

God did not remove the challenges I was facing. He strengthened me to face the challenges and to discipline myself to do what needed to be done to overcome those challenges.

God's grace was more than enough for me and His grace is more than enough for whatever challenge you may face.

So, go ahead and shout it out – I Am Weak! and watch God's power over your life.

Declaration: Declare today, Lord I am weak! Your grace is all I need.

Action: Study God's Word. Meditate on scriptures on God's grace and strength.

Prayer: Lord, I am weak. I am no longer ashamed of my weaknesses and will speak proudly of them. You my Father will meet me at my points of weakness and make me strong with Your power. In Jesus Name. Amen

I Can Do All Things

For I can do everything through Christ, who gives me strength.
Philippians 4:13

Paul was thanking the Philippians for their gifts. He was telling them that although he may not have had much, he had learned to be content with what he had.

Paul was shipwrecked, imprisoned, whipped, beaten, stoned and persecuted. Paul had learned, what I needed to learn - I don't need super human powers. I do not have to be wonder woman. Christ gives me the strength to do all things and to handle everything.

Throughout my season I was trying to be all things to everyone, do all things for everyone, solve every problem that came my way. I stressed whenever an issue came up. I cried when a bill was due. I was juggling many balls in the air and killing myself to keep any from hitting the ground.

When I anchored and started to have a personal relationship with Christ, I begin to understand how Christ strengthens me. There will always be challenges, problems, and pressures. But Christ provides me the strength to face those things that come my way. The strength to be patient; strength to stop before speaking; strength to think before being impulsive; strength to seek Him always.

Declaration: Declare today, I can do all things through Christ who gives me strength.

Action: Study God's Word. Meditate on *Philippians 4:10-20-God's Provision (ESV)* and *2 Corinthians 11:16-33-Paul's Many Trials (NLT)*.

Prayer: Lord, in all I do I seek Your guidance and Your strength. Like Paul I will face many trials. And like Paul through You Father, I can do all things as You strengthen me. I may not have much Father, but I thank You for what I do have. In Jesus Name. Amen

God's Strength

The LORD gives his people strength.
The LORD blesses them with peace.
Psalm 29:11

T his scripture is the last verse of *Psalm 29.*

I can look back in my season and see where God strengthened me to continue on.

When I faced a hostile work environment, it was God who strengthened me to face each day.

Psalm 29-Ascribe to the Lord Glory (ESV) speaks of the power of God.

His voice echoes above the sea.
His glory thunders over the mighty sea.
His voice is powerful.
His voice is majestic.
His voice strikes with bolts of lightning.

In this Psalm of David, we are learning of God's strength and power over nature. This is the same strength our Father gives to us. Strength and power over human nature.

Isaiah 40:29 tells us – *He gives power to the weak and strength to the powerless.* The strength and power I received from Christ helped me to deal with the isolation I experienced on the job.

Jesus gives strength and power to us. Jesus gives us peace. We are powerful in Jesus Name. We are freed from the drama of life with

128

the calming peace provided by Jesus. Again, God is our refuge and in that refuge is strength.

The strength God gives us helps us go on each day.

Declaration: Declare today, I am strengthened by God each day to continue on.

Action: Study God's Word. Meditate on *Psalm 29 Ascribe to the LORD Glory (ESV)*.

Prayer: Lord, thank You for the strength You give me each day to deal with the daily stresses of life. Thank You for the blessing of peace that calms my spirit. Your mercy, grace and favor are what sustains me each day. In Jesus Name. Amen

Be Strong and Courageous

This is my command – be strong and courageous! Do not be afraid or discouraged. For the LORD your God is with you wherever you go.
Joshua 1:9

The LORD is speaking to Joshua after Moses' death and charging him to lead the Israelites. God promised Joshua as He promised Moses, to be with him wherever he goes. To protect him and not abandon him.

This scripture is the third time within this passage that God is commanding Joshua to "be strong and courageous".

As I anchored in God's Word I could look back onto the early years of my season and see where God had made me strong and courageous. Strength both physically and mentally. When my body felt as if I just wanted to curl up and not move – He strengthened me to rise and face another day. When mentally I just could not deal with one more issue – He gave me clarity to understand and make decisions. When fear gripped me of not knowing how I would move forward with the bankruptcy – He gave me courage to face my responsibility as the sole owner of the property.

I realized I was the leader of my own situation. I had to be strong and courageous. I had to let go of fear and trust that God was with me.

Even though I was not with God in my early season, God was with me. He heard the cries of my heart even if I did not cry out with my voice. As God was with Moses and Joshua – He was with me.

God is with us in all places. Be determined, unwavering, fearless, bold. No anxiety, no sorrow.

Stay rooted in Christ. Steadfast and true. No fear. Fear has no place in our relationship with God.

Declaration: Declare today, I am strong and courageous in God. Fear has no place in my relationship with God.

Action: Study God's Word. Meditate on scriptures on being strong and courageous. Study Joshua on how he obeyed God's commands to lead the Israelites to the Promised Land.

Prayer: Lord, thank You for making me strong and courageous. I let go of my fear and I trust that You are with me always. As I face any situation, I will stay rooted in Christ. You are with me in all I do. Fear has no place in my relationship with You. In Jesus Name. Amen

Suit Up

*Put on all of God's armor so that you will be able to stand firm
against all strategies of the devil.*
Ephesians 6:11

We are in a daily battle with the enemy for our spiritual life.

The enemy will use every tool at his disposal - family, friends, coworkers, social media, movies, music, magazines, etc. The list is endless.

The enemy will disguise his tactics as - friendly gossip, an innocent lie, self-doubt, mistrust, anger, fear, busyness (you know what I mean - "I'll just skip church this Sunday" "I'll catch up on bible study") He will attack at all hours of the day and night. He is active 24/7, 365 days of the year.

We are not alone in this battle. As my mother would say - Oh, what a God we serve! God has provided us with the armor needed to stand, fight and defeat anything and everything the enemy throws our way.

Fasten on the **Belt of Truth** to defeat the lies of the enemy.

Put on the **Breastplate of Righteousness** to protect our hearts against self-doubt, mistrust, etc.

Put on the **Shoes of Peace** and continue to spread the gospel of God and doing the work of Christ.

Take up the **Shield of Faith** to protect us from the arrows of temptation thrown at us.

132

Put on the **Helmet of Salvation** to protect our mind from all doubt.

Take up the **Sword of the Spirit** - staying in God's Word, committed to Prayer.

When we are clothed in the Armor of God we are not just protected, we are also covered with Grace and Mercy.

Declaration: Declare today, I am suited up in the Whole Armor of God.

Action: Study God's Word. Meditate on *Ephesians 6:10-20 The Whole Armor of God.*

Prayer: Lord, I thank You for clothing me with the Armor. Your armor helps me to fight against the attacks of the enemy and to stand true in Your Word. Your armor helps me to be a guardian of faith. With Your armor, I do not fight alone – I fight with grace and mercy. In Jesus Name. Amen

Protection, Peace and Victory

The LORD is my light and my salvation; whom shall I fear? The LORD is the stronghold of my life; of whom shall I be afraid?
Psalm 27:1 (ESV)

This is my mantra scripture I say it every day. I say it whenever I need to calm my nerves, hold my tongue, revive my spirit.

Fear, anxiety, worry. These are words that imprison us. We all have felt fear – fear of rejection, fear of sickness, fear of loss, fear of death. We feel anxiety and worry over our health, finances, relationships, etc.

We can become so paralyzed in fear, so overcome with anxiety and worry that we lead ourselves down the path to illness, hopelessness, depression. Why are we afraid? Why do we worry? Why do we fill ourselves with paralyzing anxiety?

Fear, anxiety, worry - these are words that are not in God's vocabulary.

We can conquer these feelings. We conquer fear with confidence and trust in God. We conquer anxiety with the calming Peace of Christ. We conquer worry with faith in God.

It is hard. I have stumbled. I have felt fear, anxiety and worry. But when we walk with God, we are under God's cover. And when those feelings appear - speak this scripture, seek God's face and declare Victory!

Victory over fear - Victory over worry - Victory over anxiety. Pray it, speak it, declare it!

134

Declaration: Declare today, I have protection, peace and victory in Christ. Fear has no place in my walk with Christ.

Action: Study God's Word. Meditate on *Psalm 27 The LORD Is My Light and My Salvation (ESV).*

Prayer: The Lord is my light and my salvation; whom shall I fear? The Lord is the strength of my life; of whom shall I be afraid? Lord, thank You for freeing me of fear and anxiety. By Your grace I walk in victory. In Jesus Name. Amen

Wisdom

For the LORD grants wisdom!
From his mouth come knowledge and understanding.
Proverbs 2:6

Ask for Wisdom

If you need wisdom, ask our generous God, and he will give it to you. He will not rebuke you for asking.
James 1:5

James is providing this advice in his letter to persecuted Christians. Speaking on faith and endurance. If you need wisdom, ask God for it. He will not be disappointed because you asked him.

Proverbs 2:3-6 tells us of *The Value of Wisdom (ESV)*. How to receive it, how to store it and how to seek it.

yes, if you call out for insight and raise your voice for understanding, if you seek it like silver and search for it as for hidden treasures, then you will understand the fear of the LORD and find the knowledge of God. For the LORD gives wisdom; from his mouth come knowledge and understanding.

As I anchored myself in God's Word, I came to understand the wisdom I sought and that God provides is not just knowledge. It is the wisdom to understand. The wisdom to make the right choices. The wisdom that would guide me through my difficult season and life.

When I went through the hostile work environment, God gave me wisdom without my asking. I did not directly pray for wisdom but God knew that in that moment I needed wisdom. His wisdom. God's wisdom guided me in not making the emotional, knee jerk reaction of leaving my position. The wisdom to take the problem to those in leadership. The wisdom to respect God's direction and trust his resolution of the problem.

Jesus teaches us about asking, seeking, and pursuing God in *Matthew 7:7 – Keep on asking, and you will receive what you ask for. Keep on seeking, and you will find. Keep on knocking, and the door will be opened to you.*

Christ is telling us don't give up in any situation. Keep pursuing God and ask him for what is needed – wisdom, patience, understanding, strength.

Declaration: Declare today, I have wisdom, patience, understanding and strength from God.

Action: Study God's Word. Meditate on *Proverbs 2 The Value of Wisdom (ESV)*.

Prayer: Lord, thank You for giving me wisdom. I will not give up! I will ask and keep asking for what I need to make it through difficult situations. You are a generous God who gives me wisdom, knowledge, patience and understanding. I will not give up! In Jesus Name. Amen

Stop Judging Yourself

Do not judge others, and you will not be judged.
Do not condemn others, or it will all come back against you.
Forgive others, and you will be forgiven.
Luke 6:37

Here Jesus is teaching about judging others. But this scripture spoke to me about judging myself.

In my season of struggle, I felt judged for wrong decisions. I felt condemned and unforgiven. And all those feelings were my own. I was prosecutor, judge and jury.

Human nature tests our actions. Each day we can stand in judgment over others for the littlest of things. We also stand in judgment of ourself. Self-harming is not limited to physical harm. The spoken word has enormous power. The unspoken word has enormous power. We criticize and berate ourself with words and thoughts. We can tear down or build up ourself with a simple word or thought.

This scripture spoke to me and helped me to stop self-harming myself with negative thoughts. God had not judged me. I judged myself. God had not condemned me. I condemned myself. God had forgiven me, but I could not forgive myself.

No more self-harming! Stop judging yourself!

Declaration: Declare today, I release all negative thoughts and stop self-harming myself with words. I forgive myself of past deeds.

Action: Study God's Word. Meditate on *Luke 6:37-42 Jesus Teaches about Judging Others*

Prayer: Lord, thank You for not judging me. Thank You for not condemning me. Thank you for forgiving me. Teach me Lord to stop self-harming myself with negative thoughts and words. I can be my own worst critic. Teach me to forgive myself for my past deeds, and to let go of the past. Help me to move forward in the life you have for me to lead. In Jesus Name. Amen

Be Still

"Be still, and know that I am God!
I will be honored by every nation.
I will be honored throughout the world!"
Psalm 46:10

W hen I study on this scripture, it speaks to me in two ways. First as a Child of God to be still and know that He is my Father. Second as a Child of God to know my place and humble myself.

Psalm 100:3 tells us: *Acknowledge that the LORD is God! He made us, and we are his. We are his people, the sheep of his pasture.* He is our creator, our Father. We belong to Him. He is our Shepherd. We are covered with His hedge of protection. He's our rock, our sword, our shield. Be still. Remain calm. Be silent. Understand God is all-powerful over-all nations, heaven and earth. He can and He will fight our battles.

We are children of God – we are NOT God. *Isaiah 2:17* tells us pride and arrogance of man will not stand. We will be humbled and the LORD alone will be honored and praised. Our service in God's Kingdom is to bring Him the Glory. We are to spread the word of the Good News of God's Kingdom, not boast of our works.

To God be the Glory!

Declaration: Declare today, I am a Child of God. I lift Him up and give God the praise!

Action: Study God's Word. Meditate on *Psalm 46 God Is Our Fortress (ESV)*

Prayer: Lord, I lift You up and give You praise. Thank You for the many ways in which You are my Father. I still myself and know that You are God. My God. I humble myself in service to You. In Jesus Name. Amen

Tell Your Problem About God

But true wisdom and power are found in God;
counsel and understanding are his.
Job 12:13

I learned a very valuable strategy during the second half of my season. Talking to my problem.

We are always telling God our problems. But God already knows what we are going through. We need to start telling our problem about God.

Tell of God's wisdom and power. His good judgment, advice, guidance, support, strength.

Job 9:4 tells us: *For God is so wise and so mighty. Who has ever challenged him successfully?* In simple words – Do not challenge or test God. God does not break and run from anyone or anything. His wisdom and strength are unmatched.

Imagine that conversation:

Problem: I'm bringing storm clouds your way.

Me: In the past your storms would bring me stress and worry. Not anymore.

Problem: You are going to have difficult days ahead. There will be tears.

Me: Okay send the storm. My Father will calm the sea and collect my tears in His bottle.

Problem: But the storms I am sending are massive.

Me: Send your storms. They will pass over. My Father does not break and run. He already knows what is coming because You can't send anything my way without Him. He is all knowing and all powerful. He has counsel and understanding. He strengthens me when I am weak and builds me up when I am torn down. He provides me with guidance and gives me good judgment to handle anything that comes my way.

Tell your problem about God. And watch God deal with it.

Declaration: Declare today, I will tell any and all problems about the power of God.

Action: Study God's Word. Meditate on *2 Corinthians 4:8-9.*

Prayer: Lord, I may have troubles, but I am not crushed. I may be confused but I will not lose hope. I may be harassed, but not abandoned by God. I may get knocked down, but I am not destroyed. I stand on the true wisdom and power I have in God. In Jesus Name. Amen

No Going Back

So you must live as God's obedient children. Don't slip back into your old ways of living to satisfy your own desires. You didn't know any better then.
1 Peter 1:14

"You didn't know any better then." Focus on that. Make it personal. "I did not know any better then."

In the 1st half of my season, I knew of Christ, I did not know him. I did not have a personal relationship with him. I was drifting and being tossed by storms coming my way. As I re-anchored in God's Word, I started building that personal relationship with Christ.

When I accepted Christ and committed my life to him, I was called to holy living. That means being obedient. Following the teachings of Christ. Living life in honor to God.

Romans 12:2 tells us: *Don't copy the behavior and customs of this world, but let God transform you into a new person by changing the way you think. Then you will learn to know God's will for you, which is good and pleasing and perfect.*

Our transformation begins with God changing our thinking. When our thinking is changed, we start the process of changing inwardly. As we change inwardly, our character starts to change and our actions and behaviors change to show our dedication and commitment to God.

Now that I strive to live as a child of God, I cannot go back to stupid actions of past behavior. There is no going back to the ways of the world. It is a challenging but rewarding life to lead.

146

Declaration: Declare today, I am transformed by God. My way of thinking is changed. I no longer follow the world – I follow Christ.

Action: Study God's Word. Meditate on *1 Peter-Book of Encouragement*

Prayer: Lord, I am Your child. Holy Spirit teach me to live in obedience to God. Help me to say no to the ways of the world and follow Christ. Father, I am transformed by You. The way of the world is not my way. I submit and commit my life to Christ. He is the way, the truth and the life. There is no going back for me. In Jesus Name. Amen

AFTERWORD

I Came Through the Storm

When you go through deep waters, I will be with you When you go through rivers of difficulty, you will not drown. When you walk through the fire of oppression, you will not be burned up; the flames will not consume you. Isaiah 43:2

Notice the scripture states "when" – not if. You will go through storms in life. But whether that storm is of water or fire – God will be with you.

When you are knee deep in a season, it is very difficult to see God's movement. You are so focused on surviving you have no thoughts of thriving.

While I was in my season, I could not see what God was doing. I did not see where God was active in each situation and working it out on my behalf. It was not until I started studying God's Word and building a personal relationship with Christ that I began to see His work in my season.

Reading the Bible for me was always difficult. I could not fully understand scripture. When I went back to anchor myself – my mother told me – "do not read the bible, study and meditate on God's Word. Ask God to open your eyes to see, your ears to hear, your mind to understand and your heart and soul to receive."

What a difference! Studying God's Word, I discovered that -

Like Shadrach, Meshach and Abednego - I could feel the heat of my struggle. But Christ was with me in the fire. (*Daniel 3:19-30 The Blazing Furnace*)

Like Daniel – I may have been fed to the lions, but I was not eaten. (*Daniel 6 Daniel in the Lions' Den*)

Like the Disciples facing a fierce storm. I was tossed by wind and waves but Jesus calmed the storm. (*Luke 8:22:25 Jesus Calms the Storm*)

God brought me through the storms and fire and out of my season of struggle. I came through the fire and was not consumed. I walked out on the other side without the aroma clinging to me. And now is not the time to stop. Now is the time to take up my cross and soldier on in my new season.

A season of Learning and Development.

Learning to forgive. Learning to love. Learning to trust. Learning to be faithful. Learning to serve. Learning to honor God. Learning to follow Christ. Learning to press in to the Holy Spirit.

Developing my spiritual gifts. *A spiritual gift is given to each of us so we can help each other. 1 Corinthians 12:7 (1 Corinthians 12- Spiritual Gifts*).

Developing myself with the Fruits of the Spirit. *But the Holy Spirit produces this kind of fruit in our lives: love joy, peace, patience, kindness, goodness, faithfulness, gentleness, and self-control. Galatians 5:22-23.*

Throughout my career I attended numerous conferences and there was always a speaker that would ask "What would you do if you were not afraid?"

Today I challenge you to think – "What would my life be like if I confessed my sins and submitted and committed to Christ?

Psalm 34:8 tells us - *Taste and see that the Lord is good. Oh, the joys of those who take refuge in him!* Think of the scene in Mary Poppins when Mary and the children are taking the same medicine from the same bottle and each experiencing tasting something different.

That is what happens when you read God's Word. That is what happens when you commit your life to Christ. That is what happens when you say Yes to God. What you experience with God will be different than what others experience. Yes, we all receive love, mercy, grace, favor, salvation. However, we receive it uniquely designed for us because we were uniquely designed by God.

When I confessed my sins, accepted Christ, and submitted my life to Him the fog started lifting, the seas calmed, the storm clouds rolled away. Faith replaced fear. Trust replaced anxiety. Love replaced hate. Peace replaced chaos. Hope replaced despair. Joy replaced sorrow. And Prayer and Fasting became two of the most powerful disciplines in my life.

As I began to understand that my assignment from God was to shares scripture that walked me through my season, I ignored, deflected and rejected. However, God had other plans. He placed me in places where I would receive direct confirmation from His chosen vessels that "Yes, this is your assignment and My Will to be done."

Even with the confirmations, I resisted. I pulled out my last argument as to why I could not write and share my story – I was too old. So, God threw at me what He knew would get me – His Word.

Genesis 6:14 – Noah was over 500 years old when called to build the Ark.
Genesis 17:4 – Abraham was 99 years old when he made the Covenant with the Lord.
Genesis 21:2 – Sarah was 90 or 91 when she birthed Isaac.
Exodus 3:2 – Moses was 80 years old when called by God to lead the Exodus.

His message was received – If I can call others in advanced age, I can call you!

I thank God for giving me this assignment and placing His trust in me to follow through.

I pray that the sharing of scripture will help someone who is struggling to understand that – you are not alone; you are loved; you are worthy; you are a daughter/son of the King.

I encourage you today to anchor yourself in God's Word. Do not read the Bible like a novel. It is not. Go into studying God's Word with expectation. Expecting to be refreshed, renewed, restored. Expecting to increase your faith, trust, hope and joy. Expecting to receive knowledge, wisdom and understanding. Expecting to draw nearer to God. Expecting to see, hear, feel, and taste the goodness of God.

I encourage you to start building a personal relationship with Christ. Christ tells us in *John 14:6* He is the way to God. *Jesus told him, "I am the way, the truth, and the life. No one can come to the Father except through me."*

My personal veil was torn and I now have a personal relationship with Christ. God was with me and walked me through the storms of - bankruptcy, health issues, broken relationships, financial struggle, loss of family. And as God was with me – He is with you!

Remember – when you anchor yourself in God's Word, you are anchoring yourself in Christ. *John 1:1-2*

In the beginning the Word already existed. The Word was with God, and the Word was God. He existed in the beginning with God.
John 1:1-2

Declaration: Declare today, God is with me always. I am a daughter/son of the King. Christ is my Lord and Savior.

Action: Study AND meditate on God's Word. Confess your sins, submit and commit your life to Christ. Talk to God. Build your personal relationship with Jesus Christ.

Prayer: Lord, I confess my sins and accept Jesus Christ as my Lord and Savior. Lord, I tear my veil to have a personal relationship with

You. I commit my life to You. I accept the Holy Spirit as my helper and mentor and invite Him into my temple. I commit and submit myself to the commandments and principles of the Kingdom of God. In Jesus Name. Amen

ABOUT THE AUTHOR

Alice R Owens is a Woman of God, a Disciple of Jesus, a Temple for the Holy Spirit. A new writer and Christian Blogger who is passionate about studying God's Word, and currently working on publishing a book series sharing Scripture to help others get Anchored in God's Word.

Please visit her website at https://www.anchoredingodsword.com/ to sign up for emails about new releases in the Anchored in God's Word book series.

You can connect with Alice on
Facebook: www.facebook.com/groups/anchoredingodsword/
Twitter: https://twitter.com/AliceOwensWOG
Instagram: https://www.instagram.com/anchoredingodsword/
Website: http://www.anchoredingodsword.com

GOD BLESS

www.ingramcontent.com/pod-product-compliance

Lightning Source LLC
Chambersburg PA
CBHW071442090426

4273 7CB0001 1B/1756